# THE PATH ALCHEMICAL OF YOGA

## SEVEN STAGES TO LIVING COHERENCE

By

Tracy Shearer

Dr. Enolia Harris Pedro

Enolia International Publishing
Cover design by Tracy Shearer



info@enolia.live | www.enolia.live

Info@flourishwithtracy.com |www.flourishwithtracy.com

# DEDICATION

This book is dedicated
to every soul who entered yoga seeking relief
and stayed long enough to meet
transformation.
To those who felt something awaken that no
one explained.
To those whose practice quietly dismantled
who they once believed themselves to be.
To those who did not turn away
when the path shifted from comfort into fire.
To the elders—named and unnamed—
who carried these sciences in breath, bone,
sound, and silence long before they found their
way into books.
And to the future initiates,
who will step onto the mat not to escape the
world,
but to learn how to enter it with clarity,
courage, and coherence.
May this work meet you
at the exact gate you are ready to cross

# INVOCATION

We invoke the intelligence that breathes
through all forms.
We invoke the geometry that holds the stars
and the spine alike.
We invoke the fire that refines without
destroying, and the silence that teaches
without words.
We call upon the lineages of light and shadow,
of earth and sky,
of body and cosmos, of number and flame.
May what be read here not remain as concept.
May it descend into nerve and marrow.
May it rearrange the hidden architecture of
perception.
May it awaken what is true, and dissolve what
no longer serves.
Let this book be a threshold. Let this reading be

an initiation.

Let those who enter do so willingly. Let those who pass through be changed.

What they have always been, now remembered.

# STAGES OF ALCHEMY

- **Nigredo** (Blackening)

*The stage of dissolution and breaking down. It is where the old structures are decomposed, and the initiate enters the void of transformation.*

- **Albedo** (Whitening)

*The stage of purification and circulation. Here, the initiate learns to breathe, refine, and allow clarity to emerge.*

- **Citrinitas** (Yellowing)

*The dawning of inner structure and pattern. This stage reveals the geometry and order within consciousness, making the hidden architecture visible.*

- **Rubedo** (Reddening)

*The stage of ignition and embodiment. Fire enters the blood; the heart becomes the furnace, and the initiate learns to carry the charge of will and truth.*

- **Cauda Pavonis** (Peacock's Tail)

*The blossoming of multiplicity and color. This*

*stage unveils the spectrum of possibilities, revealing the many paths and correspondences within the one light.*

- **Distillation**

*The refining and narrowing down. After the multiplicity of Cauda Pavonis, this stage is about focusing the essence into a singular, potent direction.*

- **The Philosopher's Stone**

*The final integration and embodiment of coherence. The initiate becomes the living synthesis of all elements—number, geometry, harmony, and cosmic consciousness—transmitting without distortion.*

# TABLE OF CONTENTS

# PUBLISHER'S NOTE

*The Alchemical Path of Yoga: Seven Stages to Living Coherence* is not a conventional yoga manual, nor does it attempt to present yoga as a system of exercise, wellness, or lifestyle enhancement. This work is offered as a **serious contribution to the understanding of yoga as an integrative discipline of consciousness**, rooted in ancient traditions and articulated for the modern reader.

The perspectives presented in this book draw from multiple streams of study and lived transmission, including classical yoga, Western alchemy, sacred geometry, cosmology, somatic intelligence, and indigenous lineages. While these traditions are often studied separately in contemporary contexts, this book brings them into dialogue in order to illuminate their shared structural principles rather than to conflate or homogenize them.

Readers are encouraged to approach this text with discernment, patience, and respect for the depth of the material presented. The practices, concepts, and frameworks discussed herein are not intended to replace professional medical, psychological, or therapeutic care, nor are they presented as prescriptive techniques to be applied without appropriate guidance. Rather, they are offered as educational and contemplative material meant to deepen understanding of yoga's transformative potential when engaged responsibly.

This book invites thoughtful study, embodied inquiry, and personal reflection. It does not ask for belief, but for attention. It does not seek to persuade, but to reveal structure. As with all serious works rooted in traditional knowledge systems, its full meaning unfolds over time and through practice.

The publisher honors the authors' commitment to intellectual rigor, ethical transmission, and respect for lineage, and offers this work to readers who are prepared to meet it with care.

# ACKNOWLEDGMENTS


## Tracy Shearer

With a heart full of gratitude, I offer my deepest thanks to those have walked beside me on this alchemical path.

To my beloved family – **Cary G.**, the seer, the holder of truth, the one whose steadfast presence and provision has given me the space to be – to dream, study, and create; my sons, whose lives fill me with profound pride and inspiration.

To my divine feminine lineage - my daughter-in-law, granddaughters, and **Mamie Harvin Johnson**, who has led by example, thank you for embodying the sacred continuity of grace, strength, and unfolding wisdom. You remind me daily of the beauty of what is yet to come.

To my **siblings**, thank you for holding space in your own special way, and to **Sui Hong Dan**, always reliable, always present, forever sister-friend.

To my collaborator, **Dr. Enolia Harris Pedro**, thank you for your brilliance, your partnership, and your unwavering commitment to walking this path with integrity, courage, and heart. Your presence has enriched this work beyond measure.

To my fellow yogi, seeker, author, scholar, teacher, world traveler and lifelong friend, **Mark W. Aycox**, thank you for the countless conversations, reflections, and moments of truth we have shared along the way. Your companionship has been a steady light.

And to all others who have supported, encouraged, challenged, guided, or simply believed in me- teachers, students, friends, sisterhood circles, and kind souls who appeared at just the right time - please know that your energy lives in these pages. This book is not mine alone; it is the collective breath of every person who has contributed to this journey.

With love, humility, and immeasurable gratitude - thank you.

**Dr. Enolia Harris Pedro**

Words alone cannot fully express the depth of gratitude I carry for the many souls who have walked beside me, guided me, challenged me, and shaped the evolution of my life's work. Every step of my growth has been carried by the wisdom, patience, and generosity of others, and this book stands as a testament to a journey that has never been mine alone.

First and foremost, I bow in reverence and profound thanks to the **Indigenous Elders–Medicine Women and Medicine Men**—who have been entrusted into my life as teachers, guides, and spiritual anchors. With deepest humility and love, I honor **Grandmother Isabel Meawasige, Grandmother Shirley Sweet, Grandfather Lynch Archuleta, Grandmother Maria Yraceburu,** and the many other Elders who took the time to teach me, sit with me, walk with me, and share their knowing. You will never fully know the magnitude of your impact through the simple and sacred act of giving your time. Whether our moments together were brief or unfolded across many years, each exchange became a foundational stone in the living wisdom that informs this work.

I extend my deepest gratitude to **Tracy Shearer**, my trusted partner in collaboration, teaching, and inquiry. *The Alchemical Path of Yoga* is born not only from individual reflection, but from a shared devotion to coherence, embodiment, and lived wisdom. Our dialogues, teachings, and mutual commitment to integrating philosophy, practice, and consciousness have profoundly shaped both the structure and soul of this book. I am deeply grateful for your intellectual clarity, your willingness to walk the path alongside me, and your dedication to bringing this work into the world as a living teaching.

I also wish to acknowledge my colleague and fellow seeker, **Carlos Concepcion**, whose work and insights opened pathways into the Masters and mystical traditions that I may never have encountered without our collaboration. Your intellectual rigor and spiritual curiosity expanded my vision and invited me into deeper dimensions of inquiry and integration.

To my husband, **Job Pedro**, I offer my deepest gratitude and love. Your patience, steadfast support, and quiet strength have been a constant presence throughout the unfolding of this work. You have stood beside me with understanding and encouragement, holding space for both the intensity and the stillness required to bring this book into being. This journey would not have been possible without your unwavering presence.

To my sons, **Nicholas and Joseph Foti**—may you always continue to engage in deep conversations across all knowledge, remaining curious, open, and ever-seeking. May the wisdom you cultivate and carry forward live on through you as my legacy.

My thanks also extend to all those whose names may not appear on this page, yet whose presence, encouragement, challenge, or example played a pivotal role in my personal and professional formation. To those who entrusted me with the opportunity to teach while I myself was still deeply in the process of learning—your faith in me became fuel for my becoming. You allowed me to grow into responsibility through service, and for that I am eternally grateful.

From my heart to yours, thank you for walking with me, believing in me, and helping to shape the path I continue to walk

# FOREWORD

*"Believing, feeling satisfied that you know modern yoga without reading this book would be a travesty!"*

In the physical sense, without a doubt, discovering yoga was a good fit for me. And like for so many others, it took me some time to reach this conclusion. Before my initiation to yoga, I was tight and inflexible which caused me pain and discomfort – even injury. I believed the cause of this was simply due to my workouts. Only later did I consider that my emotional state could even be a factor. In the beginning, yoga helped soothe my condition. It was an exciting time; there seemed to be no limit where physical yoga could take me. That inspired me to study more, to get into meditation. Eventually, I completed an accredited course. Yet even after hundreds of hours of study, there seemed to be something else? There was something missing, and it appeared to be connected to my own personal growth. Why did I feel so lost and confused at times? Why couldn't I readily manifest the self-empowerment I required to feel whole in my environment? I had a lot of questions stored up inside of me. Yet I didn't quite know where to start looking for those answers. After reading T*he Alchemical Path of Yoga – The Seven Stages to Living Coherence* – I have felt a genuine gratitude towards the authors of this book for filling that void.

Tracy Shearer and I go back to high school during the decade of the late seventies, where we studied in an academically accelerated program. Back then, we were being prepared for university by a diverse group of passionate, dedicated inner-city teachers. After going our separate ways post-graduation, surprisingly, years later, Tracy and I reconnected through an article she wrote regarding the importance of eating raw food. After catching up, we resumed our friendship as adults.

Flash forward a decade later. When Tracy informed me that she was writing a book about yoga I was happily surprised. But when she started describing the Alchemy elements of the book to me, I assumed it might be over my head. Since reconnecting, Tracy has been a solid influence on my overall health, helping me create more flexibility in my approach. Her well-rounded skill set and diligent nature has exposed me to many different fields of knowledge. While her relationship with other talented practitioners has also influenced my life in positive ways, the co-author of this book, Dr. Enolia Harris Pedro, is a prime example of this. Dr. Pedro's resume is instantly impressive. Not only in the academic fields but also as someone who has immersed herself in cultural study all over the world. These two authors being fine examples of women dedicating their lives to helping others through their tireless efforts and projects, I was willing to give *The Alchemical Path to Yoga* a shot.

This book delivers a captivating read! Right from the beginning the authors made me comfortable. I felt confronted, awoken, and challenged all at the same time, but always respected in my pursuit of answers. The pages flowed by, as my search for the deeper meaning of my life was directly responded to. No matter where you are in your yoga timeline, *The Seven Stages to Coherence* can become a useful platform to springboard your life to rewarding new heights. These stages can be used as an insightful mirror or as a road map for self-transformation. The descriptive language is an absolute joy to read, bordering on the poetic at times, without sacrificing any of its potency. Viewing yoga only from the physical was actually limiting me. This book explains the importance of the interplay between the physical and the non-physical. Readers discover it is the consciousness that is key. They discover "why" the physical takes place, helping us have a better comprehension of the internal self.

*The Alchemical Path of Yoga – The Seven Stages to Living Coherence* offers a fresh, comprehensive opportunity to understand yoga as an integrative discipline of consciousness, rooted in ancient traditions and presented simply for the modern reader.

" *There is a human history lesson within the pages of this book that readers will never forget.*"

**Mark W. Aycox** ,

*Yogi, Writer, Teacher, Well-being Advisor*

---

**Mark W. Aycox** (b. 1963, Philadelphia) is a writer, yogi, and educator whose life bridges embodied practice and global experience. His path includes union carpentry, fashion modeling in Milan and Paris, and a decade as a personal trainer in New York City. After traveling through more than thirty countries, he earned a teaching degree in Bangkok and taught across Southeast Asia. He now lives in Pacific Mexico, where he writes and practices yoga.

https://markwaycox.github.io/author/index.html

**Where do you search me?**
I am with you.
Not in temples, nor in mosques,
not in rites or renunciation.

I am not in yoga postures,
nor in breath held tight.

If you seek me truly,
you will see me at once—

**I am the breath within the breath,**
the seer behind the seeing.

— *Kabir*

PREFACE

# Why This Book Exists

This book was born the way many true works are born—not from strategy, not from trend, not from market demand, but from a recognition that something essential had been missing for a very long time.

Tracy Shearer came to this work through the living body of yoga—through breath, posture, nutrition, rhythm, healing, and daily devotion. Her life was shaped by practice: the consistency of showing up on the mat, the discipline of teaching, the intimacy of walking beside students as they moved through change. She knew what yoga does in the nervous system, in the tissues, in the habits of a human life. She had seen people heal. She had also seen people stall. And she had begun to sense that while many were learning *how* to practice, very few were being shown *where the practice was meant to lead.*

Dr. Enolia Harris Pedro came to this work through a different doorway—through number, geometry, cosmology, sacred language, indigenous transmission, and the long arc of consciousness studies. Her life was shaped by the Trivium and Quadrivium, by the Archéomètre, by Gematria, by alchemy, by the living cosmologies carried by elders. She spent decades studying how intelligence structures itself in the universe—and how those same laws quietly shape the human being. She had seen coherence as a mathematical reality, a nervous-system reality, and a cosmological reality. And she had watched as modern spiritual culture borrowed the surface of ancient traditions while often losing their structural depth.

When these two streams met, they recognized that something essential had been missing from both worlds when held alone.

Yoga, in modern times, had become largely physicalized—fitness-driven, therapeutic, or aesthetic—often stripped of its full cosmological, mathematical, and initiatory depth. Sacred science, meanwhile, had become abstracted—studied in diagrams, symbols, and philosophical systems—often detached from embodied practice and daily human struggle.

This book was born from the realization that these were never meant to be separate domains.

We did not sit down to "design" this book in the traditional way. In truth, the book arrived before we fully understood what it was. Tracy dreamed the title before a single chapter existed. Enolia began seeing the structural layout of the work before its narrative had taken form. What followed was not so much an act of authorship as it was an act of listening.

We witnessed, again and again, that the material did not originate from us as ideas to be invented. It arrived through us as something to be translated. It felt less like creation and more like remembrance.

Between us, the body of yoga and the architecture of consciousness found a common language.
Together, we realized that what was trying to emerge was not simply another yoga book, nor another esoteric text, nor another wellness manual. What wanted to be born was a **map of conscious coherence**—a living pathway that shows what yoga is actually preparing the human being for when walked to its true destination.

## Who This Book Is For

This book is for the one who is just beginning the yoga journey—whose body is curious, whose breath is just learning to listen, whose nervous system is waking up to the idea that there is more to being human than survival and repetition.

This book is for the one who has been practicing faithfully for years—who knows the postures, the sequences, the breath ratios, the language of alignment and release—but who has quietly wondered, somewhere beneath the surface: *Is this all there is?*

This book is for the one who has mastered technique—who teaches, trains, leads, holds space— but who senses that mastery of form is not the same as mastery of consciousness.

And this book is for a fourth category that is rarely named directly in modern yoga culture:

**The initiate.**

The reader who is not merely seeking improvement, health, or even awakening—but is unknowingly standing at the threshold of a far older journey of transformation. The one whose life is already being reorganized by forces they do not yet have language for. The one who feels the fire, the pressure, the pull toward something vast—but has not been shown the map of what that pull actually means.

If you are reading this book and feel that your life itself—not just your practice—is being initiated...then this book is for you.

## Why This Book Matters

Yoga in the modern world is often framed as a wellness system, a fitness method, a mental health tool, or a spiritual lifestyle. All of these are true—but they are not complete. What has largely been lost is the understanding that yoga was originally designed as a **coherence technology**.

Not coherence as a belief.
Not coherence as positive thinking.
But coherence as a measurable, embodied state in which:

- Breath, posture, nervous system, and perception align
- Thought, feeling, action, and timing synchronize
- The human instrument becomes ordered enough to conduct higher intelligence without distortion

This book exists because that destination has not been clearly named in most yoga education. Students are taught *how to move.*

But rarely why that movement exists in the first place.

Students are taught how to breathe.

But rarely what that breath is organizing them toward.

Students are taught ethics, devotion, strength, release, and flexibility.

But rarely are they shown that all of those are

stages in a precise alchemical sequence whose purpose is the formation of a coherent being.

This book is the missing bridge between doing yoga and becoming what yoga was designed to form.

## What This Book Is Actually Doing

Rather than organizing yoga by anatomy, style, or pose families, this book is organized by the **Seven Stages of Alchemy**—because that is the deeper structure that has always guided human transformation across cultures.
Each chapter corresponds not to a fitness goal, but to a **threshold of consciousness**:

Dissolution.

Circulation.

Structure.

Fire.

Spectrum.

Distillation.

The Stone.

Within these stages, yoga is revealed not as exercise, but as a **living initiation sequence**—one that has been silently preparing the nervous system, the will, the heart, and perception for something far more consequential than relaxation or flexibility.

This book also reveals, for the first time in an accessible way for the yoga world,

the **Quadrivium**—Number, Geometry, Harmony, and Cosmos—not as medieval abstractions, but as **the living operating system of yoga itself**:

Number as the intelligence inside breath and repetition. Geometry as the intelligence inside posture and alignment. Harmony as the intelligence inside rhythm, mantra, and vibration.

Cosmos as the intelligence inside timing, seasons, cycles, and sky.

And beyond that, it introduces the **Archéomètre, Gematria, and sacred correspondences** not as esoteric curiosities, but as **maps of the very coherence yoga has been building in the body all along**.

## The Path This Book Opens

The destination of this work is named clearly:

The Path of Coherent Consciousness.

A state in which:

- The nervous system can hold intensity without fragmenting
- The heart can carry power without corrupting
- The will can act without self-betrayal
- The mind can perceive structure without falling into domination
- The body becomes a reliable instrument of truth

This path has always existed.
But it has rarely been described in a single integrated transmission that speaks simultaneously to:

The practitioner. The teacher.
The scholar. The initiate.

This book does not ask the reader to abandon tradition. It asks the reader to **complete it**.

## Their Shared Intention

Tracy Shearer brought the living body of yoga.
Dr. Enolia Harris Pedro brought the cosmological and mathematical anatomy of coherence.

One dreamed the field.
One recognized its structure. Together, the work assembled itself.
They did not set out to create a book that fit neatly into any existing category. They set out to create the book they both wished had

existed decades earlier—the book that would have shown where yoga actually leads when it is allowed to complete its original purpose.

If this work brings new meaning to practice...
If it reveals patterns that have long been felt but not yet named... If it steadies the fire that has already begun to move inside life...
Then it has done what it came here to do. And now, reader—

**the initiation is no longer only on the page.**

It is within you.

## INTRODUCTION

# THE INVITATION TO BECOME

Most people believe they come to yoga for the body. They come because of pain, stress, tension, fatigue, aging, injury, or restlessness. They come because something feels tight, heavy, inflamed, or misaligned. They come because they want to feel better, calmer, stronger, more flexible, more at home in themselves. And yoga, in its great compassion, meets them exactly there—because the body is the only doorway most human beings can feel at first.

But yoga has never been a system designed for the body alone. The body is simply where the deeper work becomes unavoidable.

What is actually being initiated in yoga is not muscle, not breath, not posture, not even mind in the ordinary sense. What is being initiated is the **capacity of human consciousness to become coherent inside matter**—to survive truth without distortion, to hold intensity without fragmentation, to carry structure without rigidity, to burn without corruption, to translate between inner and outer worlds without losing center.

This is why those who stay with yoga long enough eventually realize that what is happening to them cannot be explained by fitness alone. Their nervous system changes. Their emotional range deepens. Their relationships reorganize. Their values rearrange themselves. Their will sharpens. Their tolerance for self-betrayal collapses. Their life begins to move as though guided by something more precise than preference.

Yoga is not simply helping them feel better.

It is quietly **reassigning the way reality moves through them**.

Every authentic sacred science has described this reassignment in different language. Alchemy called it the Great Work. Mystery schools called it initiation. Hermeticism called it alignment between worlds. The Quadrivium called it learning how reality is structured through number, geometry, harmony, and cosmos. Yoga called it union. None of these were separate paths. They were separate vocabularies for the same interior event: consciousness learning how to survive in matter without lying to itself.

This book exists because modern yoga culture rarely speaks this truth plainly. It teaches breath, but not what breath eventually awakens.

It teaches flexibility, but not what flexibility ultimately dissolves. It teaches focus, but not what focus eventually ignites.

It teaches peace, but not the fire that inevitably follows peace when peace becomes real.

Thousands of yoga books already exist. They teach how to align the hips, how to sequence a flow, how to calm the mind, how to strengthen the core, how to open the heart. But very few speak directly about what all of this is preparing you for. They show you techniques without revealing the **consequences of success**.

Because when yoga truly works, it does not simply relax you. It reorganizes you.

And this reorganization follows a pattern that human beings have encountered across continents and epochs, long before yoga was ever named as such. In Africa, in India, in China, in Mesopotamia, in the Celtic forests, in the deserts of the Middle East, in the tundra of the far North—human beings entered altered states through posture, heat, rhythm, silence, starvation, fire, sound, and ordeal. The outer forms differed. The inner sequence did not.

There was always dissolution. Then purification.

Then structure. Then ignition. Then multiplicity. Then refinement.

Then—only when the human vessel could finally carry it without shattering—coherence stabilized as the Stone.

India did not invent this sequence. India preserved it. Yoga became one of the most precise carriers of this universal initiatory arc, encoding alchemy into breath, posture, discipline, devotion, and sound so seamlessly that the practitioner could be transformed without ever being shown the entire map at once. The body would be taught first. The nervous system second. The will only much later. And the full consequence of what was happening would often only become clear when it could no longer be avoided.

This book restores that missing architecture. Not to intellectualize yoga.

Not to make it more complex.

But to make it finally **honest about what it does**.

This is not a book for those who want yoga only as exercise. It is not for those who want transcendence without responsibility. It is not for those who want light without shadow, softness without fire, or power without purification. It is for those who have already felt that something irreversible is happening through their practice and have not been given language for it.

You may have arrived at yoga because your body hurt.

You may have stayed because your breath began to feel strange in unfamiliar ways.

You may still be practicing because your life no longer fits inside the person you used to be.

If so, this book is not introducing you to a new

path.

It is showing you the full depth of the one you are already walking.

Here you will not be asked to master yoga as a system.

You will be asked to recognize what has already begun to master you.

You will be shown why stagnation had to come before circulation. Why circulation had to come before structure.

Why structure had to appear before fire. Why fire had to awaken before multiplicity.

Why multiplicity must be distilled before coherence can stabilize.

You will see that your breath was never just breath. Your posture was never just posture.

Your mantra was never just sound. Your will was never just personal. Your timing was never random.

Yoga has always been number made flesh, geometry moving through bone, harmony vibrating through nerve and voice, cosmos turning inside blood and choice.

This book is not meant to be rushed. It follows the order in which the nervous system actually learns to survive truth. Some chapters may feel like recognition. Others may feel like confrontation. Others may feel like a remembering that happened long before your education gave it a name.

Let that happen.

This is not a book to finish. It is a book to enter.

Every real sacred science begins the same way. Not with light. Not with answers. Not with power. But with dissolution. With thaw. With the moment when what has been frozen can no longer hold.

The ancient alchemists called this Nigredo. The yogic traditions simply led the initiate into the dark and taught them how to breathe there.

Your journey begins in the same place every real journey begins— With the courage to let what is frozen finally melt.

And so, we begin in black.

# CHAPTER ONE

# NIGREDO

*"Most of us arrive at yoga because something hurts. We don't always realize that the pain is not a problem to fix, but a threshold asking to be crossed."*

— ***Tracy Shearer***

*"Nigredo is the sacred descent into the Void of Emptiness—the place where all false forms collapse, where identity is stripped of its disguises, and where consciousness stands with nothing left to hold but truth itself."*

— ***Dr. Enolia Harris Pedro***

Most people enter yoga the way a block of ice enters water.

Solid. Dense. Already shaped. Already carrying the history of every temperature, it has survived.

They arrive with their personalities forged, their habits calcified, their stories hardened into identity. They arrive with grief compressed into the hips, fear braced into the ribs, vigilance locked into the jaw. They arrive with beliefs frozen into certainty and memory packed into muscle. And they call this "who I am."

But what they are feeling is not identity. It is **stuckness**.

Yet beneath this stuckness lives something quieter and far more powerful than discomfort:

a **yearning**. A longing not merely to feel better, but to **know more**, to **become more**, to touch the deeper capacities of awareness that have always whispered beneath daily life. The initiate does not come to yoga only because life is painful. The initiate comes because something inside begins to ask for **consciousness itself**—not as concept, but as lived reality.

This is why the path begins. Not because the body needs stretching, and not because the mind needs calming — but because something in the deeper intelligence recognizes that frozen structures cannot carry living consciousness forward.

Yoga enters life not as movement first, but as **thaw**.

Yet here is where modern understanding has quietly inverted the ancient law. Most people believe the sequence is: move the body, and the mind will follow. Stretch the muscle, and consciousness will soften. Adjust the posture, and perception will reorganize.

But the old traditions knew something different. The true ice is not in the muscle.

It is in the **state of mind**.

Long before posture was formalized, initiates entered through **mental dissolution**. The physical body served only as the mirror that revealed what the mind was gripping. The poses were never

the primary work — they were the evidence that the inner work had begun to destabilize the old structure.

This is the alchemical secret of Nigredo.

Nigredo is not simply darkness. It is not punishment. It is not depression wrapped in spiritual language. Nigredo is the moment when the internal temperature changes just enough that solidity can no longer pretend to be permanence.

The initiate does not enter yoga to become flexible. The initiate enters to become **unstuck**.

And unstuckness is first a **psychic condition**, not a physical one.

The mind freezes around survival. Around memory. Around protection. Around inherited pattern. Around trauma that has been renamed "normal." Over time, these patterns take on mass. They become heavy. They become rigid. They become familiar enough to feel like truth.

To yearn for consciousness is to feel, however faintly, that this rigidity is not the full architecture of being.

This is where discipline first appears—not as punishment, but as **permission to change state**. The initiate begins to adopt form deliberately: practices of movement, of restraint, of nourishment, of attention. The asanas enter not as gymnastics, but as **listening instruments**. The Yamas and Niyamas enter not as moral commandments, but as the **first tools of honest self- inventory**. Nutrition shifts not as ideology, but as the first recognition that what we consume becomes who we are. The inward turn begins quietly, almost awkwardly, in a world trained to look outward first.

This first turning inward is the **first face-to-face encounter with the Void**. Not the Void as annihilation.

But the Void as **capacity**.

The Void is what appears when distraction softens. It is what opens when the external world no longer dictates the entire field of awareness. It is not shadow itself—but the **space in which shadow and light can finally be seen**.

This, too, is Nigredo.

The initiate begins to notice where the body is stuck — and in the same breath, begins to recognize where consciousness has been **narrow**, where it has refused certain truths, where fear has drawn its invisible borders. The tight hip is not just muscle. It is a history of avoidance. The collapsed chest is not just posture. It is unexpressed grief holding its breath. The rigid jaw is not just tension. It is restraint rehearsed for survival.

here, for the first time, the mirror is honest.

Nigredo is the first inventory of self that does not lie. Yoga does not confront this with argument.

It introduces **heat**.

But this heat is not aggression. It is not forcing. It is not striving. It is the subtle internal friction that begins when awareness is reintroduced to sensation. When breath is reintroduced to presence. When movement is reintroduced to consciousness rather than performance.

As the thaw begins, what was once silent begins to move. Not as story at first – but as sensation.

Tremor. Temperature. Pulse.

Release.

This is why the earliest yogic traditions did not begin with form. They began with **state**.

Long before there were lineages, manuals, schools, studios, certifications, or philosophies arranged into neat hierarchies, human beings were already entering altered conditions of awareness. These were not practices learned from teachers. They were responses to awe, terror, mystery, grief, longing, wonder, and the overwhelming presence of the living cosmos. The earliest yogic moment was not a posture. It was the sudden collapse of ordinary perception under the weight of something vast.

Before yoga had a name, it had a function:

to help consciousness survive encounters with infinity.

Early humanity did not ask how to stretch the

body. They asked how to remain sane when lightning split the sky, when the sun disappeared and returned, when birth opened portals between worlds, when death arrived without warning, when dreams spoke in symbols sharper than daylight. The question was not flexibility. The question was **how to orient consciousness inside a universe that was clearly alive and incomprehensibly vast**.

So, the first yogic technologies were **states of consciousness**.

Silence.

Vigil.

Rhythm.

Breath suspension.

Star-gazing trance.

Fire-watching.

Drumming.

Fasting.

Isolation.

Solar exposure.

Darkness retreats.

These were not cultural inventions. They were **neuro-cosmic responses**—ways to regulate the shock of being human inside a living galaxy.

As civilizations emerged, these primordial state-arts were preserved by priesthoods, initiatory orders, and mystery schools. What had begun as raw survival intelligence became **sacred science**.

In the Kemetic temples, the initiate was first unthreaded from identity through silence and solar disorientation. The inner compass was broken open by shifting light, long ceremonial durations, and symbolic death passages. Before any movement was taught, the initiate's sense of personal time was dismantled. One learned first how to *disappear into cosmic rhythm.* Only later did posture appear—as a way to stabilize a consciousness already loosened from its former shape.

In Taoist internal alchemy, the practitioner did not begin by shaping the body. They began by returning awareness to the **embryonic field**—the state before breath was divided into effort and rest, the state before personality defended itself against sensation. This was not metaphor. It was a neurological reversion to pre-egoic organization. The goal was not improvement. It

was recovery of original coherence.

In Hermetic chambers, matter itself was treated as a stand-in for the psyche. Substances were sealed, broken down, dissolved, calcined, and reconstituted as external mirrors of internal transformation. The human being was never seen as separate from this process. Before recombination, there was always **decomposition**. Before ascent, always descent. Before light, always blackness.

In ecstatic trance cultures across the planet—from Africa to the Americas, Siberia, and the ancient Mediterranean—the body was pushed past ordinary rhythm through drumming, prolonged movement, breath exhaustion, and fasting until the everyday identity simply could not hold its structure. The shaking, the visions, the collapses—these were not performances. They were **failures of the old self to contain expanded consciousness**.

None of these traditions began with "improving the body." They began with **breaking the spell of the ordinary mind**. Form came later. Form came as a stabilizer, not a doorway.

Only once consciousness had learned how to melt, dissolve, loosen, and reorganize did structured movement arise as a way to **give shape to what had already shifted internally**. Posture was not the entrance. It was the scaffold that allowed the initiate to remain functional after radical perception had already begun.

This is the inversion that modern yoga forgot.

Over time, as civilizations became more rigid, as social order replaced cosmic order as the primary organizing principle, yoga gradually moved from **state-first** to **form-first**. What had once been designed to regulate altered consciousness gradually became recast as philosophy, religion, fitness, therapy, lifestyle.

And yet, the pressure that created yoga in the first place never disappeared.

When India received these teachings, it did not invent yoga. It **systematized it**—translating cosmic state-knowledge into an internal method that could be practiced within everyday human life. The fire altars moved from stone to breath. The sacrifice became attention. The star chambers turned inward and became the subtle body. The heavens entered the nervous system.

India performed one of the great translational acts of human history: it turned **cosmic initiation into personal realization**.

By the time Patanjali codified the Yoga Sutras, thousands of years of state-based exploration had already been distilled into a precise inner architecture. Ethics stabilized the vessel. Posture made the body breathable. Breath made the mind permeable. Withdrawal freed attention.

Concentration restored direction. Meditation reopened the field. Absorption rejoined the observer with the observed.

Yet even here, the original truth remained quietly encoded:

Yoga was still about state, not shape.

The modern nervous system still mirrors this ancient landscape.

The thunder of prehistoric skies has become the electric hum of devices. The fire rites have become deadlines. The drum rhythms have become schedules, alarms, and notifications. The disorientation once induced by stars now arrives through information overload and chronic stimulation.

The environment has changed. The **nervous system has not**.

It still freezes under pressure. It still narrows under fear.

It still contracts around uncertainty. It still armors itself through control.

And so the same ancient condition returns: Consciousness freezes.

The initiate no longer enters through desert ordeal.

The initiate enters through burnout, grief, illness, anxiety, numbness, quiet despair, and the un-nameable sense that something essential has been lost.

The threshold did not disappear. It simply changed location.

And it is here that the disciplines of yoga return to their original purpose.

Asana reappears not to sculpt the body, but to **locate where perception has frozen into posture**. The Yamas and Niyamas return not as imposed morality, but as **thermodynamic ethics**

—ways of regulating the internal environment so thaw does not become collapse. Nutrition returns not as ideology, but as **phase-appropriate fuel for transformation**. The inward turn becomes the most radical act of all in a civilization addicted to outward validation.

Nigredo is not an ancient relic.

It is the living condition of every sincere human being who longs for consciousness but has not yet learned how to become fluid again.

And so the initiate stands exactly where initiates have always stood: At the edge of what has been constructed.

At the threshold of what must dissolve.

At the meeting place between who they have been

and what they are just beginning to remember how to become. This is why this first stage is necessary.

Not because one must suffer to awaken.

But because nothing frozen can carry living consciousness forward.

The journey ahead will not be about force. It will be about **phase transition**.

From solid to liquid. From liquid to radiant. From fixation to flow.

From identity to intelligence.

And this begins not when the body touches the mat — but when the mind allows itself to **melt**.

## CHAPTER TWO

# ALBEDO

## Whitening · Circulation · Breath as Bridge

*"When I first began to understand breath, I realized it wasn't just something I was doing—it was something that was doing me. Every inhale arrived like a quiet teacher. Every exhale carried a lesson I didn't yet have language for."*

— ***Tracy Shearer***

*"Albedo is the moment when the thaw learns how to move. Breath becomes the governing intelligence that teaches consciousness how to circulate without drowning, how to feel without collapsing,*

*and how to live inside sensation without losing the Self.”*

— ***Dr. Enolia Harris Pedro***

When ice melts, it does not vanish. It becomes water.

Nigredo dissolves what was frozen, but it does not yet teach the initiate how to move what has been freed. The first shock of thaw brings sensation rushing back into territories long abandoned by attention. Feeling returns before meaning does. The nervous system begins to register again. And with this return comes vulnerability—the raw exposure of circulation after long stagnation.

Albedo is the stage that follows melting. If Nigredo is the breaking open,

Albedo is the learning how to breathe inside the opening.

This is the whitening—not as purity through

denial, but as clarity through circulation.

Here, the initiate discovers that thaw alone is not enough. Without guidance, without rhythm, without coherence, thaw can become flooding. Old emotion pours out without boundary.

Sensation overwhelms. Memory erupts. The body releases, but the mind does not yet understand how to remain present inside the release.

This is where breath enters not as accessory, but as governing intelligence.

Long before breath was counted, shaped, measured, engineered into ratios, or arranged into named techniques, it was recognized as the first law of life moving through form. Breath is not merely the exchange of gases. It is the only system in the human being that belongs simultaneously to volition and surrender. You can command it, yet it will continue without your will. You can shape it, yet it also shapes you. It is the only bridge where conscious intention and autonomous life meet and agree to cooperate.

This dual nature makes breath the original negotiator between identity and infinity.

When ancient observers watched living beings, they recognized something unmistakable: wherever there was breath, there was animation; wherever breath departed, form collapsed back into earth. Breath was not seen as movement within life. Breath was seen as the signature of life itself entering and leaving form. To breathe was to host intelligence. To stop breathing was to release it.

In Albedo, the initiate learns this bridge not as concept, but as direct nervous-system experience. Breath becomes the means by which thaw is circulated without disintegration. It is what carries sensation without overwhelming it, what allows feeling without drowning, what permits memory to move without fragmenting identity.

The earliest breath practices on Earth were not designed for comfort. They were survival technologies for altered states.

When human consciousness first began to loosen its allegiance to the ordinary sensory field– through trance, fasting, isolation, prolonged rhythm, deprivation, solar exposure, or ecstatic movement—the primary danger was not revelation. It was loss of tether. The psyche could travel faster than the body could stabilize. Vision could expand faster than coherence could regulate.

Ecstasy could outrun integration.

Breath became the anchor that made inner flight survivable. It regulated trance so that it did not tip into psychosis.

It stabilized vision so that it did not dissolve into fragmentation. It kept the body inhabitable while perception traveled beyond it.

In Kemetic ritual science, breath was understood not as personal respiration but as solar fluid— the rhythmic loan of Ra inside human form. To inhale was to receive sunlight in invisible form. To exhale was to return what had been borrowed. The lungs were not merely organs; they were solar gates. The cadence of breathing aligned the initiates' nervous system with the rising and setting of the Sun, synchronizing human interior time with stellar time.

In Taoist internal alchemy, breath was the river of original essence. Through breath, the jing was protected, the qi circulated, and the shen clarified. Breath conserved coherence. It prevented essence from leaking out through scattered attention. It allowed intelligence to spiral, condense, and distill.

In Hermetic physiology, breath was the

invisible solvent. Just as mercury dissolved metals without destroying their essence, breath dissolved psychic density without destroying integrity. It carried subtle fire without burning the vessel. It thinned emotional coagulation so that light could pass through without distortion.

In shamanic trance traditions, a change in breathing was often the first sign that the boundary of the ordinary world had loosened. Before visions appeared, before trembling began, before voices arrived, the breath shifted. The tribe recognized immediately what was occurring: consciousness was changing environment.

Only later, in the Indian translation, did breath become method.

Pranayama was not invented to calm the mind. It was systematized to govern transformation.

As breath became operative rather than

automatic, it revealed that it is not a single movement but a fivefold intelligence. Respiration differentiates into five major currents of organization known as the Five Vayus—five expressions of how life force circulates through body, psyche, and awareness.

Prana Vayu gathers inward. It governs inhalation, sensory intake, and the movement of awareness from the periphery toward the center. Neurologically it corresponds to parasympathetic cranial and upper thoracic regulation. In Albedo, Prana teaches consciousness how to receive without scattering.

Apana Vayu moves downward. It governs elimination, detoxification, release, and the psychic capacity to let go. Neurologically it corresponds to pelvic and sacral autonomic circuitry. In Albedo, Apana prevents circulation from becoming congestion and teaches the system how to release without collapse.

Samana Vayu equalizes. It governs digestion and assimilation on every level. Neurologically it aligns with the enteric nervous system and gut-brain integration. In Albedo, Samana teaches the initiate how to digest experience rather than drown in it.

Udana Vayu moves upward. It governs expression, memory, speech, insight, and ascent of awareness. Neurologically it corresponds to higher vagal branches, brainstem, and cortical activation. In Albedo, Udana teaches consciousness how to rise without dissociation.

Vyana Vayu distributes. It governs circulation, coordination, and integration across the entire organism. Neurologically it corresponds to the global somatic nervous system and circulatory coherence. In Albedo,

Vyana ensures that transformation does not fragment into isolated releases but becomes a unified field.

Prana receives.

Apana releases.

Samana digests.

Udana elevates.

Vyana integrates.

Together, the Five Vayus form the circulatory geometry of Albedo.

Modern physiology now speaks of vagal tone, autonomic balance, enteric intelligence, cortical regulation, and locomotor integration. Yogic science speaks of the Vayus. These are not opposing models. They are different languages for the same living intelligence.

In Albedo, the initiate begins to feel these

currents directly. They notice when breath gathers in the chest instead of the belly. When release stalls in the pelvis. When digestion fails to convert emotion into nourishment. When insight rises too quickly without grounding. When energy scatters instead of circulating.

This sensitivity is the return of bio-energetic literacy.

Through breath, the initiate enters dialogue with the autonomic self. The nervous system begins to teach its own laws. The breath becomes a feedback instrument. What overwhelms can be modulated. What stagnates can be mobilized. What fragments can be integrated.

And as breath refines, something even subtler begins to emerge. Breath begins to resonate.

At first this resonance is barely perceptible—a quiet hum beneath the lungs, a subtle tone in the throat, a delicate vibration along the spine.

Over time the initiate realizes that breath is never silent. The skeleton hears it before the ears do. The nervous system resonates before the voice forms sound.

This is where sound is born directly from breath, not as chant yet, but as internal vibration. When breath becomes steady, rhythm appears.

When rhythm stabilizes, proportion emerges. When proportion repeats, number awakens.

This is the hidden bridge between Albedo and Citrinitas.

The breath intervals begin to self-organize. The system begins to find its own harmonic ratios without force. The being begins to tune itself from within.

Breath is no longer only oxygenating blood. It is tuning the human instrument.

This is why Nada Yoga never truly begins with the voice. It begins when breath becomes audible to awareness. The mantra is silent at first. Its geometry assembles inside the rib cage, along the spine, inside the pressure gradients between chest and skull.

Albedo is the threshold where circulation becomes resonance.

This is the whitening: transparency to vibration. Distortions thin. The nervous system conducts frequency instead of resisting it. The initiate does not become free yet—but becomes transparent enough for light to begin passing through.

And where light can pass through without distortion, structure inevitably appears.

Now prepares perception for pattern. Pattern prepares perception for geometry. Geometry prepares perception for number.

And thus, without effort, without imposition, without doctrine, the next stage reveals itself.

Where circulation stabilizes,

structure awakens.

And this is where the golden threshold of the work begins.

And yet, breath does not remain only circulation.

Once resonance stabilizes, once the nervous system no longer resists vibration, breath begins to press gently against the boundary of audibility. What was once only internal hum approaches the edge of sound—not as speech, not yet as chant, but as a subtle tonal presence hovering just beneath the voice.

This is not the introduction of mantra. It is the approach of mantra.

At first, nothing is vocalized. The initiate simply becomes aware that breath itself has tone. Each inhale carries a faint pitch. Each exhale carries a dissolving echo. The throat becomes a listening chamber before it becomes an instrument. The body hears itself before it ever speaks.

This is how sound is born correctly in the work. Not imposed.

Not performed.

But discovered as the audible edge of vibration already alive within the breath.

The nervous system begins to register that breath is not only movement—it is oscillation. Not only circulation—it is wave. And as this realization stabilizes, the first shapes of breath quietly announce themselves.

The first is the **circle**.

Inhalation arcs outward. Exhalation returns inward. There is no sharp beginning. There is no true ending.

Breath becomes a continuous loop of return. The psyche begins to release its obsession with linear time. The initiate no longer experiences effort as a straight line of striving but as a field of rhythmic continuity.

From the circle emerges the **triangle**.

Inhale.

Pause.

Exhale.

Three distinct phases. Three internal positions of consciousness—reception, suspension, release. This is the first appearance of number inside the body, not as arithmetic, but as experienced order.

And once the triangle begins to move, it does not return as a circle.

It unfolds as a **spiral**.

Breath no longer simply repeats. It advances.

Each cycle does not return to the same depth. Each return arrives altered. The same inhale enters a different interior landscape. The same exhale carries a different density of release. The spiral is the sign that transformation has gained direction.

At this stage, subtle sounds may begin to arise spontaneously—a hum without intention, a quiet tone without language, a vibration in the sinus cavities or the chest. These are not yet mantras. They are pre-phonetic signal tones—the nervous system testing how vibration moves when it is no longer resisted.

This is the embryonic phase of Nada Yoga. Not sound practiced.

But sound approaching consciousness. It is here that the initiate first senses:

**"I am not only breathing.**

**Something is beginning to speak through my breath."**

This is the precise moment where Albedo reaches its inner crest. Circulation has become resonance.

Resonance is becoming vibration. Vibration is preparing to become form.

Breath no longer only governs sensation.

It begins to hint at structure beneath sensation. And this is the true threshold.

Not yet geometry. Not yet number.

But the unmistakable awareness that structure is about to reveal itself.

The initiate now stands at the edge of a new kind of perception— where breath will soon be seen,

where vibration will soon be mapped, where sound will soon organize space, and where the golden clarity of form will rise from within the body itself.

And thus, without rupture, without doctrine, without force, the alchemical work turns toward its next luminosity.

**Citrinitas is near.**

# CHAPTER THREE

## CITRINITAS

*Yellowing · Structure · The Dawning of Pattern*

*"There comes a moment when the body realizes it is not improvising anymore. Every movement begins to feel guided by something that was already there."*

— ***Tracy Shearer***

*"Number is how balance feels from the inside. Geometry is how the body remembers who it is. And when these awaken together, the soul discovers that it has always been standing inside a living pattern."*

— ***Dr. Enolia Harris Pedro***

When structure first appears, it does not announce itself as mathematics. It arrives as recognition.

After the whitening of circulation, after breath has learned how to move without freezing and resonate without flooding, perception begins to change in a way that is almost imperceptible at first. The initiate does not suddenly "see geometry." What begins to emerge instead is a subtle but undeniable awareness that experience itself is organized.

Something is shaping sensation from within.

The mind notices that breath no longer moves randomly. It follows invisible arcs. The body feels that movement is no longer chaotic; it follows quiet pathways. The nervous system begins to sense that vibration is no longer diffuse. It is arranged.

This is Citrinitas.

Not illumination as vision.

But illumination as pattern becoming visible inside living motion.

This is why the ancients named this stage the yellowing, the dawning of gold—not the final fire of Rubedo, but the first recognizable gleam of order inside transformation. It is the moment when consciousness realizes that it is not moving through an abstract mystery—it is moving through a crafted intelligence.

Here, the initiate no longer experiences breath only as circulation. Breath now appears as ratio.

The pauses between inhale and exhale no longer feel arbitrary. They begin to take on shape. The length of breath begins to prefer certain proportions. The body begins to settle into rhythms that feel inevitable rather than chosen.

This is not discipline yet. It is discovery.

The initiate begins to sense that breath is teaching number from the inside. Not as counting.

Not as measurement imposed. But as proportion felt.

This is how number enters consciousness correctly—not as abstraction, but as the grammar of experience itself.

The earliest yogic seers did not "invent" number. They recognized that nature already counts. The heart counted before mathematics named it. The lungs counted before ratios were written. The tides counted before calendars existed. The seasons counted before gods were carved.

Citrinitas is the stage where the initiate begins to notice that they, too, are being counted by something far more precise than personal intention.

The first form this counting takes is the circle.

The initiate has already felt it through breath. Now it becomes visible to awareness. Every inhale returns. Every exhale completes. The psyche begins to sense that existence is not linear striving but orbital recurrence. The circle is not repetition for its own sake—it is coherence moving through time.

From the circle arises the recognition of the center. And with the center comes the first quiet question:

“If there is a center, what fixes it?”

This is the birth of axis inside perception.

Once axis appears, the second form emerges naturally—the line.

Not a line drawn on paper, but a felt directive inside movement. The spine begins to register itself not as a stack of bones but as a vector.

Ascending and descending are no longer metaphorical. They become sensed directional intelligences.

The initiate begins to feel:

"I do not merely move. I am being oriented."

This is the moment where internal space becomes legible.

From circle and line, a third form emerges without being taught—the triangle. Breath has already prepared it:

Inhale. Pause. Exhale.

Three phases. Three corners. Three orientations of consciousness—reception, suspension, release. The initiate realizes that life is no longer happening in undifferentiated flow. It is unfolding in triadic rhythm.

This is the first true appearance of structure inside awareness. From here, geometry no longer remains outside the body.

The body enters geometry.

Movement begins to reveal angles. Stillness

begins to reveal symmetry. Weight reveals proportion. Balance reveals invisible lines of force. The initiate may not yet name it, but they feel it:

"There is architecture inside me."

This is where yogic posture begins to transform in meaning. Asana ceases to be shape for flexibility.

It becomes position inside a living diagram.

A forward fold is suddenly more than stretch—it is arc returning to center. A backbend is no longer effort—it is radius expanding from axis.

A twist is not just detox—it is the crossing of internal vectors. The body becomes a geometric instrument.

Not because geometry is imposed upon it, but because geometry is what has always been organizing it beneath sensation.

This is why ancient yogic postures mirror stellar forms, solar arcs, and planetary pathways. They did not mimic nature. They remembered what the body already was.

Citrinitas is the stage where this remembering becomes conscious. Number now begins to show its deeper identity.

Not as quantity.

But as quality of relation.

Two is no longer "two things." Two reveals polarity, mirroring, tension, and dialogue. Three reveals generation, stability, and synthesis. Four reveals enclosure, foundation, orientation in space. The initiate no longer experiences numbers as neutral. They begin to feel them as behaviors of reality itself.

This is the quiet awakening of the arithmetic of consciousness, though it is not yet taught as such.

At the same time, sound begins to reorganize.

The hum that arose at the end of Albedo now begins to seek proportion. The initiate notices that certain tones stabilize the breath. Others agitate it. Certain pitches calm the nervous system.

Others awaken it. The body begins to respond to sound as if it were spatial instruction.

Sound is no longer heard as decoration. It is felt as architecture in vibration.

This is why mantra does not yet become language here. It becomes geometry you can hear.

The initiate may begin to sense that a tone "opens" the chest at a precise angle. That another tone "descends" through the spine in measured steps. These are not imagined effects. They are the nervous system responding to ratio embedded in frequency.

Tone becomes a line. Interval becomes a distance.

Harmony becomes a form you can inhabit.

Now the golden nature of Citrinitas becomes unmistakable. Light no longer appears only as metaphor.

It begins to appear as intelligibility itself.

The initiate begins to see patterns in their own

movement, repetitions in their own resistance, symmetries in their own fears. Even suffering begins to reveal hidden order. The psyche is no longer drowning in experience. It is reading experience.

This is the dawning of perceptual gold.

Not because the initiate has mastered reality.

But because reality has begun to reveal its syntax.

At this stage, the initiate often feels both exhilarated and destabilized. There is sudden clarity, yet not yet full embodiment. There is recognition, yet not yet command. There is structure, yet not yet fire.

This is exactly as it should be.

Because Citrinitas does not complete the work. It reveals the map.

The body now knows it is a diagram. The breath now knows it is a ratio.

The sound now knows it is a structure.

The psyche now knows it is moving through an ordered cosmos. But the initiate has not yet become that order.

That is the work of the next fire.

Because seeing gold is not the same as becoming gold.

## The Unspoken Curriculum: When Modern Yoga Meets Citrinitas

For many who arrive at this stage through modern yoga, there is a quiet shock of recognition.

Because suddenly, what once felt like "just alignment" begins to reveal itself as something far more deliberate. The familiar instructions return with new meaning. The cues you once followed mechanically now speak in an older language—one that was always embedded in the practice, though rarely named.

You remember being told to "root through the four corners of the feet."

You remember being asked to "lengthen the spine," to "draw the navel inward," to "stack the joints," to "fix the gaze," to "balance the weight evenly," to "hold the breath in this ratio."

At the time, it sounded practical. Anatomical. Therapeutic. Technical. But here, in Citrinitas, a different realization dawns:

You were never only being trained in posture. You were being trained in form.

## Warrior II

Take Warrior II. You were told to widen your stance, bend the front knee, extend the arms, and gaze forward. It felt athletic. It felt grounding. It felt empowering. But unspoken beneath those cues was a deeper invitation:

A horizontal line through the arms—the horizon.

A triangular base through the legs—the first stable plane.

A vertical axis through the spine—the unseen column between earth and sky. A directional gaze—a vector of intent drawn into space.

Without being told, your nervous system was learning how to stand inside line, triangle, axis, and polarity all at once.

You thought you were building strength. You were learning geometry through flesh.

## Tree Pose (Axis Mundi)

Tree Pose, too, was never simply balance. You were told to root and rise simultaneously. It felt like poise and stillness. What was actually being installed was the experience of the central axis

—the living world-tree inside your own body.

Tree Pose is the embodied experience of the *axis mundi*—the cosmic pillar around which worlds turn.

One leg drills downward into the Earth as a singular root. The spine ascends as a unified vertical staff.

The crown reaches upward in directional alignment.

Tree Pose installs the central pillar again and again: one leg roots, the spine ascends, heaven and earth meet in bone and breath.

## Downward Facing Dog

Downward Facing Dog teaches the inverted triangle: force returning through distributed load rather than muscular struggle.

Hands and feet form the base. Hips rise into

the apex.

The spine stretches as a diagonal conduit between worlds.

Here the nervous system learns that geometry can carry weight with elegance instead of force.

## Cobra

Cobra becomes the arc of ignition: the pelvis anchors, the spine curves into rising fire. Curvature allows force to multiply rather than dissipate. Heat ascends without strain. Awareness climbs without effort.

The serpent awakens not as symbol but as trajectory of rising force through matter.

## Fish Pose

Fish Pose reveals the bridge: crown to earth, chest to sky, throat suspended between truth and silence. It teaches the initiate how to hold opposing forces without collapse—how to live as the keystone between worlds.

These are not symbolic metaphors. They are **mechanical mysticism**.

Triangles distribute. Arcs generate.

Lines transmit. Spirals evolve.

## The Living Grid

Beneath the postures, beneath the breath, beneath even movement itself, another intelligence is quietly organizing the body.

It is not muscular. It is not skeletal.

It is not even neurological in the ordinary sense.

It is **geometric awareness distributed through flesh**. This is the Living Grid.

The Living Grid is the invisible lattice through which force travels, perception anchors, and transformation stabilizes. It is how the body becomes readable to consciousness—not symbolically, but mechanically. Once Citrinitas awakens, the initiate begins to sense that the body is no longer a mass of parts. It is a **mapped field**.

This is where the deeper technologies of yoga reveal their true function.

**Bandhas** are no longer experienced merely as muscular engagements. They become **nodes on a vertical staff of force**—fixed points along the central axis where energy is sealed, redirected, contained, and pressurized. Each bandha establishes a geometric fulcrum inside the spine where current can change direction without escaping the vessel.

Mula Bandha anchors the lower gate so that force does not leak back into unconscious gravity. Uddiyana Bandha lifts pressure upward into circulation rather than collapse.

Jalandhara Bandha fixes the upper gate so that ascending force does not dissipate into chaos.

Together, the bandhas transform the spine into a **segmented column of containment**, allowing charge to rise without fragmentation. This is not metaphor. This is **internal engineering**.

**Drishti**, too, undergoes a transformation here. It is no longer merely where the eyes look. It becomes the **anchoring of perception on an internal grid**. When the gaze stabilizes, awareness pins itself into a location within space. The eyes no longer chase movement—they **fix reference**. Through drishti, perception learns how to hold orientation under motion without scattering.

The initiate discovers that where the eyes dissolve into wandering, the nervous system fragments. Where the gaze stabilizes, **coherence follows**.

**Twists** now reveal their deeper structure. They are no longer understood as detox alone. Twists are **crossings of force**—torsion fields generated when opposing vectors interpenetrate inside the body. One side of the spine rotates forward while the other rotates backward. This creates an internal shear where stagnation is not merely released, but **repatterned through opposing geometries**.

Twists teach the initiate how contradiction reorganizes rather than destroys. They are the spatial experience of paradox resolved through structure.

**Backbends**, too, shed their superficial identity

as "heart openers." In the Living Grid, backbends are understood as **arcs of expansion**—curvatures that multiply current rather than merely stretch tissue. Straight lines transmit force. Curves **amplify** it. Every backbend trains the nervous system how to **carry greater voltage through curved pathways without rupture**.

This is why backbends awaken emotion, courage, fear, vulnerability, and will all at once. They are not emotional postures. They are **force-amplifying geometries**.

Even **forward folds** reveal new dimension. They are no longer only surrender. They are **return arcs**—conscious collapses of the vertical axis back into containment. They teach force how to descend without losing coherence.

Every category of movement becomes a **geometric operation**:

Standing postures establish axes

Balances refine nodal stability

Twists generate crossing vectors

Backbends amplify arc-force

Inversions redistribute gravitational load

Seated postures stabilize field coherence

As this awareness deepens, the initiate realizes something both humbling and awe-inducing: The body is not simply **doing** yoga.

The body is acting as the **carrier medium for an invisible spatial intelligence**. This is why none of this was originally explained.

Because if explained too early, it would have become conceptual instead of **neurological**. The tradition trusted embodiment over explanation.

You were not taught geometry. You were **converted into it**.

And once the Living Grid is perceptible,

something irreversible occurs in the practitioner's awareness:

Movement is no longer random. Stillness is no longer empty.

Posture is no longer posture.

It is placement inside a lattice of force and meaning.

At this stage, the initiate no longer feels like a person "moving through space." They feel like **space moving through them**.

This is why Citrinitas is the awakening of structure—not on paper, not in thought, not in diagrams—but as a **felt, living, navigable reality inside the nervous system itself**.

And once the grid awakens, once force begins to travel through mapped pathways rather than chaotic discharge, the initiate becomes capable of something that was impossible before:

They become capable of **holding charge**.

And the moment a being becomes capable of holding charge—

**fire becomes inevitable**.

## Ancient Lineages Beyond India

This hidden curriculum did not originate in India alone.

Long before yoga was named, before sutras were composed, before lineages were formalized, the human body was already being trained as a **cosmic instrument** across the ancient world. What later appeared as "postures," "breath," and "discipline" were first understood as **acts of alignment between human form and celestial order**.

In **Kemetic Egypt**, initiates were not taught philosophy first. They were placed inside **light, stone, and direction**. Temples were built as stellar receivers. Bodies were positioned according to solar risings, cardinal points, and precise angles of illumination. The spine was aligned with the Djed pillar—the living symbol of vertical stability between worlds. Posture was not exercise. It was **terrestrial astronomy**. When an initiate stood, knelt, bowed, or lay in the chamber, their body became a **living hieroglyph**, written directly into the geometry of the cosmos. Breath

synchronized with the rising of Ra. Motion followed the procession of the stars. This was yoga before yoga—alignment as **cosmic function**.

In **Sumer and Mesopotamia**, posture was integrated into lunar and planetary ritual. Kneeling, prostration, suspension, and extension were performed not for devotion alone, but for **timing the human nervous system into resonance with celestial**

**mechanics**. The body learned to bow with Saturn, rise with Jupiter, kneel with the Moon. Movement was clocked by the heavens. The initiate did not pray to the cosmos—they **moved with it**.

In **Indigenous ecstatic traditions** across Africa, Siberia, the Americas, and the Pacific, bodies were shaped not through linear postures but through **spiral, tremor, suspension, collapse, and rhythmic eruption**. The axis was not taught—it was entered through trance. The spiral was not diagrammed—it was danced. The initiate learned how consciousness exits and re-enters the body through **breath interruption, sound saturation, and rhythmic disorientation**. These were not cultural performances. They were **technologies of perception**, teaching the nervous system how to survive dimensional crossing.

In **Taoist internal alchemy**, practitioners

stood for hours in postures that modern eyes would barely recognize as "doing" anything at all. Knees softly bent. Spine elongated. Crown lifted. Pelvis subtly rooted. Breath drawn into the cauldron of the lower belly. Here, the body was trained as a **vertical conduit between Heaven and Earth**. Posture was not for mobility. It was for **cosmic continuity**—so that qi could rise without escaping and descend without collapsing.

In **early Greek initiatory traditions**, long before philosophy became abstract, the body was trained through **oriented stance, measured walking, sacred stepping, and rotational movement**. The labyrinth was walked not only as a symbol, but as a **neurological encoding of spatial intelligence**. Movement trained perception to recognize recursion, return, polarity, and center.

In **Celtic and Druidic transmission**, posture and breath were shaped by landscape:

standing against wind, kneeling in water, lying upon stone, spiraling in forest clearings. The body learned geometry not from diagrams but from **horizons, solstices, river bends, and star paths**. The initiate did not learn alignment in a hall. They learned it from **earth itself**.

Across these civilizations, the truth was the same:

The body was never treated as an object to be improved. It was treated as a **threshold between dimensions**.

Then, in India, something extraordinary happened. India did not invent these laws.

India preserved them.

India gathered what had been scattered across the ancient world and **encoded it into a system that could survive time without losing its initiatory depth**. Where other civilizations lost their bodily sciences to conquest, abstraction, or erasure, India tucked the same technologies into:

Ethics (Yamas and Niyamas)

Breath (Pranayama)

Posture (Asana)

Focus (Drishti)

Gesture (Mudra)

Sound (Mantra)

And did so in a way that allowed the practice to continue **even when its original cosmological language went silent**.

This is why a modern practitioner can step onto a mat with no knowledge of Egypt, Tao, Sumer, or the stars—and still be initiated.

Because the technology is **in the body itself**.

By the time an initiate reached the end of what we now call **Citrinitas** in any of these ancient systems, the elders were no longer assessing belief, obedience, or discipline.

They were assessing capacity.

Can this body carry alignment without rigidity? Can this breath transmit force without distortion?

Can this nervous system hold charge without disintegration? Can this consciousness endure ignition without fracture?

This is what the ancient lineages were secretly preparing for. Not posture.

Not peace.

Not self-improvement.

But the **ability to survive embodiment of power**.

And that is why, across cultures, the same threshold always followed:

Once structure was established, once breath was refined, once geometry awakened in perception

**Fire came next.**

## Preparation for Fire

By the end of Citrinitas, the ancient elders were no longer testing devotion. They were testing capacity.

Could this vessel hold structure without turning rigid? Could it sense number without becoming enslaved?

Could it carry coherence without collapsing under fire? Because now the initiate is no longer a student.

They are a **combustible vessel**.

They have survived dissolution (Nigredo). They have mastered circulation (Albedo). They have awakened structure (Citrinitas).

Now gold begins to heat. Breath grows warmer.

Sound grows denser.

The heart begins to beat not only with life—but with direction.

Geometry can no longer remain cool. Pattern must become power.

Perception must become incandescence.

Light prepares to enter blood.

## Number as Living Balance

**Number is how balance feels from the inside.**

Even Surya Namaskar—approached now as fitness by many—is still a planetary ritual: A living solar orbit traced by the human spine.

A numerical devotion repeated in 12, 27, 54, 108. A human body becoming counted by celestial law.

Bandhas became nodes on a vertical staff.

Drishti became the anchoring of perception on an internal grid. Twists became crossings of force.

Backbends became arcs of expansion.

None of this was explained because the tradition trusted embodiment over explanation.

And now—here—in Citrinitas—

you are finally allowed to see what you have always been doing. You were already practicing living geometry.

## The Threshold Into Fire

At the culmination of Citrinitas, the initiate knows something irreversible: Structure exists.

Number is alive.

Geometry is not outside reality—it is what reality is doing.

But this knowing still lives in perception. It has not yet entered the blood.

The initiate can see the map.

But they do not yet burn as the map. Here, the golden clarity begins to heat.

The heart starts to feel the geometry it once only recognized. Breath grows warmer.

Sound grows denser.

Will begins to stir inside structure.

What was once pattern becomes pulse.

What was once proportion becomes pressure.

What was once harmony prepares to become force.

This is where perception can no longer remain neutral. Because truth is about to demand embodiment.

And when embodiment begins, gold must become red. Fire must enter the structure.

Light must enter the blood.

This is where geometry ignites into will, heart, and living flame.

**Rubedo approaches.**

## CHAPTER FOUR

# RUBEDO

*Reddening · Fire · Embodied Will*

*"There is a moment when the practice stops soothing and starts asking something of you. Not more flexibility—more truth. Not more balance—more courage."*

— ***Tracy Shearer***

*"Fire does not arrive to make us powerful. It arrives to reveal whether we are willing to become responsible for the power that has always been living inside us."*

— ***Dr. Enolia Harris Pedro***

*Fire Entering the Human Instrument*

There comes a moment in every real transformation when structure can no longer remain cool. Citrinitas reveals the pattern.

Citrinitas teaches the map.

Citrinitas lets the initiate see how reality is shaped.

But Rubedo demands something infinitely more dangerous. It demands that the initiate become the shape.

Until now, the work has moved through clearing, circulation, ratio, and recognition. The vessel has been purified. The breath has been tuned. Geometry has awakened. The Living Grid has locked into coherence. The initiate now knows they are not chaotic matter moving through a meaningless world—they are a precise instrument inside a living cosmos.

And still, nothing truly irreversible has yet

happened to their will. Rubedo is where that changes.

Rubedo is not the warmth of insight. It is the heat of embodiment. This is the stage where knowing enters the blood. Until this point, transformation could still be observed, described, navigated from the safety of witness. Rubedo ends observation. Rubedo begins incarnation.

The gold that was perceived in Citrinitas now drops into the circulatory system. The nervous system, once trained to perceive structure, is now required to conduct force without distortion. Breath grows warmer. Sound grows denser. The heart is no longer just the regulator of rhythm— it becomes the furnace of intent.

is why the alchemists named this stage the Reddening. Red is not merely the color of emotion. Red is the color of oxygenated blood. Red is the sign that fire has entered matter and is surviving there. Until now, transformation moved around the heart. Now, it moves through it.

The initiate begins to feel something unmistakable: a pressure behind the sternum, a brightness inside the chest that is not metaphor, a density of purpose that no longer feels like personality. This is not desire. This is direction. This is not ambition. This is alignment under heat.

Rubedo is where geometry becomes will. The lines once perceived in posture now begin to pull action into coherence. The axis once sensed becomes a spinal command. The arcs that once distributed force now amplify intention. The triangles that once stabilized now project forward into the world. What was pattern now becomes power.

This is why across all ancient traditions; this stage was never taught publicly. Because Rubedo cannot be performed safely without the three initiatory foundations already secured. Without Nigredo, fire hardens the ego instead of dissolving it. Without Albedo, fire overwhelms the nervous system instead of refining it. Without Citrinitas, fire scatters without structure instead of manifesting with accuracy. Only a vessel that has been dissolved, circulated, and structured can be trusted with ignition.

Now the initiate is no longer working toward awakening. They are working toward responsibility.

Because once fire enters the blood, nothing neutral remains. Every action becomes charged. Every word carries voltage. Every presence reshapes its field. Rubedo is not about enlightenment.

It is about consequence.

When fire enters the blood, it does not ask permission. It does not negotiate with fear. It does not wait for philosophical readiness. It arrives because the system has become capable of carrying it. This is the ruthless compassion of Rubedo. The initiate may believe that Citrinitas completed the work because perception now sees structure. But structure without heat remains blueprint. Gold without fire remains inert. The living cosmos does not transmit through diagrams—it transmits through ignition.

Rubedo is the moment when geometry is no longer merely intelligible. It becomes demand.

Where Citrinitas whispered, Rubedo commands. Where Citrinitas revealed, Rubedo requires. Where Citrinitas showed the map, Rubedo erases the option to stand outside it. Here, the initiate is no longer practicing alignment.

They are being claimed by it.

## The Nervous System Under Fire

In Nigredo, the nervous system froze. In Albedo, it learned to circulate.

In Citrinitas, it learned to organize.

In Rubedo, it learns to conduct without burning out.

This is the most dangerous threshold in the entire Great Work. Fire amplifies everything it touches. Fear intensifies into panic if the vessel is not stable. Desire swells into compulsion if it is not disciplined. Vision swerves into delusion if it is not grounded. Power tilts into domination if it is not purified by service.

Rubedo does not create these dangers.

Rubedo exposes whether they are already

present.

This is why the ancients always placed fire after structure and breath—not before. The nervous system must already know how to return to center under pressure, or fire will scatter the psyche rather than consecrate it.

Now heat begins to move through deeper currents. The solar plexus ignites as direction: a sense of inner authority that is not aggression but clear steering. The heart ignites as devotion with consequence: not sentimental feeling, but love that is willing to act. The throat ignites as truth under voltage: words thickening with gravity. The pelvis ignites as creative force and life-fire: energy that no longer wants only to discharge but to build.

What was once subtle becomes loud inside the body. The initiate may feel sudden surges of purpose that they did not crave, a need to act that does not arise from personality, creative force that arrives faster than identity can claim it, sexual energy shifting from appetite into power of generation, voice deepening in weight, decisions forming without debate. This is not restlessness. This is incarnate command beginning to assemble.

The heart, in this stage, stops being metaphor and becomes mechanism. It is not ignited in Citrinitas; it is prepared. In Rubedo, the heart becomes the living crucible because it is the only organ that can simultaneously receive, circulate, endure pressure, and direct force outward. The brain can analyze fire. Only the heart can carry it without breaking coherence. This is why across traditions the final ordeals are always heart ordeals—not emotional melodramas, but furnace ordeals: to love under fire, to speak truth under fire, to remain present under fire, to act in service under fire, to stay coherent when the entire being is electrically alive.

Rubedo does not ask, "What do you understand?"

It asks, "What can your heart carry without corrupting?"

If Rubedo is activated prematurely—before Nigredo, Albedo, and Citrinitas are stabilized—it produces spiritual grandiosity, messianic fantasy, compulsive activism, burnout framed as

service, sexual power distortions, emotional volatility justified as awakening. None of this is the fault of fire. It is what happens when voltage exceeds vessel integrity. This is why the ancients guarded Rubedo more fiercely than any other threshold—not because it was elite, but because it was irreversible once crossed. You cannot un-ignite the blood. You can only learn to govern it.

# Fire in the Body: The Yoga of Reddening

In the vocabulary of modern yoga, Rubedo is almost never named. And yet it is everywhere.

It hides beneath familiar phrases that float through studios and trainings: heat-building, power practice, strength and flow, heart openers, finding your edge, staying with the burn, activating your core, lighting up your center, awakening your Shakti, stepping into your power, standing in your truth. These are not casual metaphors. They are scattered shards of Rubedo language, spoken without initiatory context.

Rubedo appears in practice as intensity that has no clear explanation: sudden surges of heat that feel larger than exertion, emotional combustion in backbends that arrives without story, waves of shaking in long holds that are not fatigue, tears that come with no narrative attached, bursts of courage that appear unplanned, and just as often, fear of one's own rising intensity when the charge becomes undeniable.

These experiences are often labeled release, emotional detox, nervous system discharge, stored trauma leaving the tissues. All of these descriptions touch part of the truth. But what is actually happening is fire finding fuel.

Rubedo is not about flexibility.

It is about combustion inside coherence.

In Rubedo, the body itself becomes the crucible. The long-held tensions in hips, shoulders, jaw, spine, and diaphragm are no longer merely "tight muscles." They become resistive material for alchemical refinement. The deepest fears held in the solar plexus are no longer just psychological shadows. They become reactive metals waiting to transform under heat. The nervous system, once trained to tolerate sensation and sustain circulation, now enters a new phase entirely: it learns conduction under heat.

This is why postures once treated as simply "advanced" suddenly take on dangerous seriousness.

Deep backbends are no longer just heart openers. They place the cardiac furnace into direct exposure. The ribs flare. The sternum lifts. The throat becomes vulnerable. The horizon inverts. Fire moves upward without protection. Courage, grief, devotion, terror, longing, and ecstasy all rise in the same chamber because they all live in the same combustible heart-field.

Arm balances are no longer strength games. They are will tests. The body must move forward while the nervous system screams "fall." The initiate is forced to distinguish true command from reflex fear. Fire enters the will here—not as ambition, but as a new quality of inner authority.

Long warrior holds cease to be endurance contests. They become direction under sustained heat. The legs burn, the arms extend, the gaze fixes. The initiate learns whether purpose collapses when pressure grows or whether it organizes itself through fire. Many report, "I found something in myself I didn't know was there," not because they became stronger, but because their inner line refused to break.

Inversions stop being playful experiments with gravity. They reverse fire against the instinct to remain upright. Blood rushes toward the skull. Orientation dissolves. Fear ceases to be conceptual and becomes physical. The body must trust axis instead of reflex. Here the initiate discovers whether structure truly lives inside them, or whether it was only a perception held under comfort.

The body is no longer being shaped. It is being tested.

Not merely for athletic achievement, flexibility, or stamina, but for the thermal integrity of consciousness itself.

This is why practitioners become confused at this stage. They think they are just getting stronger, yet their lives begin to reorganize. They imagine they are simply advancing in practice, yet their emotions intensify. They think they are only working the heart chakra, yet their will ignites, their voice changes, their sexual energy shifts, their tolerance for self-betrayal quietly collapses.

Because Rubedo is not a chakra activation.

It is the moment when practice crosses from regulation into consequence.

Fear often arises here, but not fear of falling or pain. It is fear of one's own magnitude. The initiate begins to realize, "I am no longer just releasing what hurts. I am activating what acts." And there is no neutral fire. Once Rubedo begins, the practitioner is no longer training for peace alone.

They are being prepared for impact.

Fire in the Voice, the Womb, and the Will

When fire stabilizes in the blood, it does not remain silent. Eventually it seeks passage. The first passage it claims is the voice.

Not the polite voice. Not the trained voice.

Not the voice that knows how to belong.

But the true voltage line between inner reality and outer world.

For many initiates, this is the most

destabilizing moment of Rubedo. The voice that emerges under fire is not concerned with approval. It is concerned with alignment. Words begin to surface unedited. Truth arrives without padding. Silence becomes heavier than speech. The throat tightens not because truth is blocked, but because it has grown too large to fit inside old permissions.

People begin to say, "I don't recognize myself lately. I am too much. My words feel dangerous." Rubedo does not ask whether your truth will be liked. It asks whether it can be conducted without distortion.

Some initiates try to suppress this voice. They soften their language. They swallow their reactions. They rehearse gentler versions of what must be said and call it spiritual maturity. But swallowed fire does not become peace. It becomes pressure. Pressure in the throat becomes sickness, constriction, chronic fatigue, or sudden eruptions of sound and speech that shock even the speaker.

When fire is allowed to pass through the voice cleanly, something extraordinary happens. Speech becomes structural. Words no longer seek to persuade; they reorganize fields. Silence becomes charged with intention. Listening becomes an act of power. Ancient traditions always tied truth to fire because truth without heat is philosophy. Truth with heat becomes law in motion.

As voice ignites, fire inevitably descends deeper into the womb, the pelvis, the creative basin of life-force itself.

Here Rubedo is often misunderstood as sexual awakening. But this is too small a name for what actually occurs. What ignites here is not appetite.

It is generative authority.

Before Rubedo, sexual energy tends to seek relief, validation, union, escape, reward. In Rubedo, this current reorganizes. Desire no longer wants only bodies. Longing no longer aims only at pleasure. Attraction no longer stays personal. The same fire that once surged toward satisfaction now moves toward creation, building, birthing, mission, work, service, world-shaping. The body feels charged, but the usual outlets no longer satisfy. Old cravings lose flavor. New hungers appear that cannot be gratified by touch alone.

Creators often feel torn in this phase, caught between eros and purpose, until they realize they are not losing their sexual fire; they are being asked to scale it upward. Womb fire becomes the will to build, the urge to teach, the drive to midwife change, the compulsion to bring into form something that did not exist before. This is why Rubedo births artists, healers, architects of systems, founders of movements, initiators of new worlds. The pelvis ceases to be a site of indulgence.

It becomes a forge of futures.

Yet fire in the womb is not safe by default. If unintegrated, it becomes compulsive creation: constant projects, constant output, constant urgency without depth. If blocked, it curdles into bitterness and resentment. If externalized too early, it creates without lineage, without wisdom, without remembrance. Rubedo requires that the womb be governed by the heart, or fire will burn without knowing why it burns.

Once voice and womb are ignited, the fire must meet its final regulator: the will.

This is where Rubedo becomes unmistakable. The initiate no longer debates action in the same way. They no longer drift. They no longer tolerate half-steps without feeling the cost. Something begins to arrive beneath choice itself—a directive current.

At first it feels frightening. It does not stop to ask if you feel ready or whether this aligns with your plans. It simply moves. The initiate must decide whether to follow it or fracture against it. This is the true test of will in Rubedo: not domination, not assertion, not force, but the capacity to act without self-betrayal under heat.

A profound exhaustion often appears here—not merely physical, but the exhaustion of no longer being able to pretend. The initiate can no longer live half-states. They cannot speak partial truths without immediately feeling it in the body. They cannot choose comfort over coherence without paying for it in nervous-system currency.

The will sharpens. The timeline compresses. Delay becomes painful. Alignment becomes urgent.

Many believe at this point that they are losing control. What they are actually losing is false authorship. Rubedo removes the illusion that the personality was ever in charge. The initiate begins to realize, “I am not choosing this fire. It is choosing me.”

This is the moment where spiritual fantasy ends and real transmission begins.

From this point forward, the initiate’s life is no longer shaped primarily by preference. It is shaped by assignment: by where the fire moves, by where the pressure organizes, by where the heart can no longer remain silent, by where the future is asking to be born through this particular body.

Rubedo feels unbearable to those who still seek only peace. Because Rubedo is not about rest.

It is about responsibility for ignition.

## The Red Heart of Initiation

Before philosophy, before doctrine, before even breath refinement, fire was the universal initiator.

Not as symbol. Not as metaphor.

But as the only force capable of proving whether a human being could carry power without disintegrating.

Every ancient lineage, no matter how distant in geography or language, arrived at the same uncompromising conclusion: there is no final awakening without combustion. The question was never whether fire would come. The only question was where it would come from—and what would survive it.

In Kemetic transmission, the heart was placed at the center of the entire initiatory economy. At the moment of death—and long before death in ritual rehearsal—the heart of the initiate was weighed against the feather of Ma'at. This was never moral judgment in the modern sense. It was a pressure test. Could the heart remain coherent under the weight of cosmic law? Could it hold truth without collapsing into fear? Could it carry fire without distorting it into domination, deceit, or self-importance? The weighing of the heart was not fear-based. It was structural verification.

In Taoist internal alchemy, years—sometimes decades—were spent cultivating the lower cauldron. Breath was refined, Jing conserved,

Qi circulated, mind quieted. But the elders were never confused about the true destination. The lower center was not the goal. It was a preparatory vessel. All of this refinement existed for one moment: the instant when fire would rise and strike the heart furnace. The real test was never whether energy could be generated. The test was whether the heart could be ignited without cracking under the voltage of truth.

In Vedic transmission, Agni was not worshipped because it was beautiful. It was worshipped because it was indispensable. Agni was the eater of offerings, the transformer between worlds, the carrier of prayer into manifestation. Without fire, sacrifice remained inert. Without fire, the bridge between human and divine collapsed. Fire was not the enemy of devotion. It was its only functional mechanism.

In Indigenous ceremonial trance traditions,

fire was rarely symbolic. It was encountered through ordeal: through heat, fasting, fear, isolation, burial, drumming that dissolved time, exhaustion that shattered identity. The initiate was brought to the edge not to be punished, but to reveal whether the soul could remain intact when the ordinary structures of safety were stripped away. Fire showed what was real by burning away what was not. The elder did not ask, "Do you believe?" The elder asked, "Can you endure your own power without breaking trust with life?"

This is the key truth of Rubedo. Fire does not awaken you.

Fire shows you what awakening costs. India did not escape this reality.

India encoded it.

Rather than external ordeal, India refined the trial into internal combustion. Through tapas—sacred heat—through disciplined breath, through prolonged asana, through chanting that vibrates the heart into ignition, through bhakti that dissolves emotional containment, through karma yoga that demands selfless action under pressure, India translated Rubedo into a daily furnace.

Tapas was never about discipline for its own sake. It was the deliberate cultivation of inner heat that exposes motive. Bhakti was never about sentimental devotion. It was the practice of letting the heart burn without defense. Karma yoga was never about moral goodness. It was the demand that action remain pure under consequence. Even the injunctions against fear, attachment, and desire were not merely ethical rules. They were fire-protection laws for the nervous system under ignition.

By the time an initiate in India reached the true interior of Rubedo, the question was no longer, "Do you understand the teaching?" The question had become, "Can your heart remain true when everything in you is on fire?"

Now this same question has arrived, but without temple scaffolding, without elders at the gate, without ceremonial flames managed by priests.

In modern times, Rubedo arrives unannounced.

It comes as a life that suddenly demands truth, a calling that disrupts comfort, a creative force that no longer fits old containers, a love that burns through pretense, a grief that strips illusion, a responsibility that can no longer be deferred.

We do not meet fire in sanctuaries alone anymore.

We meet it in relationships that expose us, in careers that test our integrity, in bodies that awaken under pressure, in voices that refuse to stay quiet, in wombs that refuse to remain small, in wills that refuse to betray their assignment.

The modern question is the same ancient one, only without incense and hymn:

Can you remain coherent under ignition—or will you turn your fire into harm, avoidance, or self- destruction?

Rubedo today does not ask you to walk across literal coals. It asks you to speak truth when silence is safer, to create when hiding is easier, to stand when retreat would preserve ego, to love when fear could justify withdrawal, to serve when no one will applaud.

This is why Rubedo is still the true heart of initiation.

It cannot be outsourced. It cannot be

rehearsed. It cannot be imagined.

It can only be lived under pressure.

Rubedo is this ordeal—internalized. Not enacted in outer flames.

But in the bloodstream.

## The Weight of Fire: Accountability as the Final Trial

There comes a moment in Rubedo when the initiate realizes something that cannot be undone by thought, diluted by language, or escaped through spiritual framing. It arrives without ceremony, without announcement, and yet it changes everything.

"I am now accountable for what my

consciousness does in the world."

This recognition does not feel moral. It does not arrive as guilt or obligation. It comes as weight

—a gravity that settles into the chest and alters the way breath moves through the ribs. Until this moment, awakening could still be imagined as something personal—a journey of healing, a path of release, a private return to wholeness. But once fire stabilizes in the bloodstream and coherence holds under heat, the fiction of private transformation dissolves.

Presence itself now carries consequence. Rooms change when you enter. Conversations bend when you speak. Silence thickens when you choose not to. Attention reorganizes people without your permission or intent. The body is no longer a private instrument. It is a field generator. And there is no longer any place to hide from that fact.

This is the true crossing of Rubedo. Not the heat, not the intensity, not the power, but the sudden, irreversible realization that consciousness, once ignited, is no longer neutral.

Before this moment, one could move unconsciously and cause harm without knowing it. One could mean well and remain ineffective without feeling the cost. One could delay, deflect, and hide behind confusion. Fire strips these shelters away. The initiate begins to feel, with unsettling clarity, that every movement now registers on the fabric of others, that what once felt like personality is now operating as force, that what once felt like choice is now operating as assignment.

This is not a burden imposed from outside.

It is the dignity—and the terror—of cosmic adulthood.

Here, spirituality ceases to feel comforting. It

ceases to feel poetic. It becomes operational. The question is no longer, "Am I awakening?" The question becomes, "What does my awakening now do?"

When this realization arrives, fire must be met consciously, or it will govern unconsciously. Fire at this level cannot be suppressed. Suppressed fire does not become peace. It becomes pressure. Pressure becomes distortion. Distortion becomes self-sabotage, illness, misdirected rage, frantic creation without coherence, compassion without boundary, leadership without grounding.

Rubedo does not allow avoidance. Fire must be governed, not tamed, not worshipped, not indulged.

In the ancient world, this governance was enacted through ritual, ordeal, temple, and elder witness. The initiate was never left alone with the fire; the community itself became the containment vessel. In the modern world, that container has largely disappeared. The fire still comes, but the holding structure must now be assembled from inside the initiate's own life.

Focus becomes life-or-death at the spiritual level. Fire follows attention. Where awareness wanders, force disperses. Where awareness steadies, will vectors. The initiate begins to feel that scattered attention produces chaotic heat, while aligned attention generates directional power.

Silence becomes necessary, not as escape, but as aim. Gaze grows sacred. One-pointedness ceases to be a discipline and becomes a survival strategy for the soul.

Rhythm also reveals itself as non-negotiable. Fire without rhythm burns the vessel that hosts it. The body demands return—return to movement, to breath, to sleep, to nourishment, to the pace of earth and muscle and bone. Discipline stops being about self-control. It becomes the building of a circulatory system for fire so it does not scorch the heart from the inside.

Life itself becomes the practice. The walk becomes as important as the posture. The meal becomes as important as the mantra. Rest becomes as medicinal as effort. Without rhythm, Rubedo consumes. With rhythm, Rubedo transmits.

Yet even with focus and rhythm, the pressure must be allowed to speak. Fire trapped in silence cannibalizes the nervous system. The initiate begins to sense that voice is no longer optional. Some form of truthful externalization must occur—not for performance or confession, but for pressure release without corruption. Writing becomes unavoidable. Speaking becomes unavoidable. Singing, chanting, sounding—these are no longer aesthetic choices. They are engineering solutions for fire in the throat and chest.

Rubedo teaches quickly that truth withheld under heat becomes disease, while truth released under coherence becomes transmission.

Here the ancient and modern tests diverge. The ancients were asked to walk into consecrated flames. We are asked to walk into visibility. They were asked to endure ritual ordeal. We are asked to endure social amplification. They were asked to prove coherence before elders. We are asked to prove it under audience, speech, noise, and projection.

The modern fire does not burn through ceremony. It burns through influence—through platform, reach, and the strange alchemy of being seen.

The new question becomes sharper than the old one. Can you carry fire without turning it into identity? Can you speak without converting truth into weapon? Can you lead without turning alignment into dominance? Can you create without turning fire into self-obsession? Can you serve without turning sacrifice into currency?

Rubedo in this age does not tempt the initiate with fear. It tempts them with importance.

Importance is more dangerous than doubt.

This is why accountability is not an afterthought of Rubedo. It is the final forge.

Only when the initiate can feel, live, and breathe the truth—

I will not use my fire to escape.

I will not use my fire to dominate. I will not use my fire to perform.

I will not use my fire to abandon the work—

only then does something extraordinary occur.

The fire begins to soften without diminishing. The heat begins to refract without dispersing.

The furnace begins to lighten without losing intensity. And that is the signal.

The unmistakable turning of the Great Work.

From blaze to brilliance.

From single flame to iridescence.

From Rubedo

to the first glimmer of the Peacock's Tail.

The Transition Has Occurred

Citrinitas taught the initiate to see structure. Rubedo forces the initiate to carry it under fire.

The blood is no longer only biological. It is consecrated circulation.

The heart is no longer only emotional. It is the

central furnace of incarnation.

The will is no longer personal.

It becomes cosmic alignment expressing through human action.

Rubedo is not colorful. It is focused, single-pointed, hot, directional, uncompromising. But life is not lived in single fire alone. Once fire stabilizes in the blood and the heart learns to carry will without corruption, something extraordinary happens: multiplicity re-enters without fragmentation. This is the birth of the next world, the iridescent stage, where fire refracts into spectrum rather than consuming the vessel. Many paths can be held without confusion, many identities can exist without collapse, many dimensions of perception can coexist without psychosis, many traditions can be inhabited without betrayal.

This is not expansion backwards. This is expansion after center.

And this expansion has a name:

**Cauda Pavonis**— the Peacock's Tail—

where one fire becomes a thousand colors without losing coherence. And that is where we go next.

## CHAPTER FIVE

# CAUDA PAVONIS

*The Peacock's Tail · The Iridescence of Paths · The Quadrivium Revealed*

*"There comes a moment when the path stops looking like a straight line and begins to look like a constellation. Nothing is lost—everything is suddenly connected."*

— ***Tracy Shearer***

*"I no longer see separate traditions. I see a single intelligence speaking in many alphabets— number, breath, bone, sound, star, and symbol—each translating the same living truth."*

— ***Dr. Enolia Harris Pedro***

There is a precise instant in the Work when fire stops being singular. Up to now, everything has moved toward a center.

Nigredo took you apart. Albedo taught you to circulate.

Citrinitas revealed inner structure. Rubedo ignited your blood and will.

The whole journey has been centripetal—drawing you inward, narrowing your focus, forging a single coherent flame.

And then, without warning, something changes.

The same fire that once rose as one column of heat suddenly begins to refract.

The edges of your perception unstiffen. Colors that were once metaphor become experience. You have the unnerving sense that you are standing inside a prism, and that every part of your life is now a ray of the same light.

This is Cauda Pavonis. The Peacock's Tail.

In classical alchemy it is the moment when the matter, long worked upon, begins to show iridescent hues in the vessel. It is the sign that multiple possibilities have awakened inside a single substance. The Work is no longer only black, white, gold, or red. It blooms in blues and greens and violets. The spectrum appears.

In your body and practice, Cauda Pavonis is the moment when you realize: You are no longer walking one path.

You are standing at the crossroads of many traditions—

and all of them are speaking the same language through you. The danger here is dispersion. The gift is synthesis. The question is whether the newly revealed colors will scatter your focus, or whether they will teach you to see the one consciousness behind every hue.

This chapter is where we name, at last, what has been moving underneath your journey from the beginning:

The Quadrivium as the hidden architecture of your yoga. Number as vibration.

Geometry as posture.

Harmony as breath and mantra. Cosmos as orientation in the living sky.

And beyond that, the great wheels of correspondence - Kabbalah, Gematria, the Archéomètre,

not as exotic esoteric systems,

but as mirrors of what your practice has already made real.

You have passed through fire. Now the Work becomes spectrum.

## The Moment the Tail Opens

It rarely looks mystical when it first happens.

It looks like your bookshelf becoming confused. Yogic texts leaning against Kabbalistic commentaries. Taoist alchemy next to neuroscience. A book on sacred geometry tucked between anatomy atlases and star maps.

It looks like your practice mat becoming crowded with influences: a Surya Namaskar whispered with Sufi poetry in your mind; Ujjayi breath weaving itself with Gregorian chant you once heard in a stone church; a mudra that feels strangely Egyptian in a supposedly "purely Vedic" sequence.

It looks like your dreams filling with multiple symbols that should not coexist and yet somehow do: Hebrew letters made of light; Sanskrit bija mantras echoing through spiral galaxies; mandalas turning into wheels of zodiacal signs; your own asana practice seen from above as a moving yantra.

You have not become confused.

You have become capable of seeing more than one layer at once.

Rubedo gave you the stability to carry fire without breaking. Cauda Pavonis gives you the capacity to carry multiplicity without fragmenting.

This is the first teaching of the Peacock's Tail:

You are not being asked to choose a single color.

You are being shown that all colors belong to one light.

## The Quadrivium Steps Forward

Up to now, Number, Geometry, Harmony, and Cosmos have moved like quiet undercurrents beneath each chapter.

You tasted number in 108 cycles of Sun Salutation.

You tasted geometry in the lines and triangles of Warrior and Tree. You tasted harmony in the counted ratios of breath.

You tasted cosmos whenever practice secretly aligned with lunar and solar tides.

In Cauda Pavonis, these four no longer remain implicit. They step into the foreground as a framework.

You begin to notice that every aspect of your yoga is, in fact, speaking at least four simultaneous languages.

Number: the count of breath, the sequence of asanas, the recurring ratios of rest and effort, the pattern of days and cycles in your sadhana.

Geometry: the architecture of posture, the invisible lines of force, spirals through the spine, the mandala of your body on the mat across time.

Harmony: the rhythm of inhale and exhale, the cadence of movement, the tonal quality of mantra, the way certain chants stabilize your nervous system as if tuning a stringed instrument.

Cosmos: the timing of your practice, the felt difference between morning and night sadhana, the pull of full moon and new moon, the seasons, eclipses, retrogrades, the way sky and earth quietly set context for everything you do.

For most modern yogis, the word **Quadrivium** is unfamiliar, even though they have been living inside it. In the older Western initiatory stream, the Quadrivium was the higher path of learning: four sacred arts that trained perception rather than opinion. Number taught the initiate to feel reality as pattern. Geometry taught them to see structure in space. Harmony taught them to hear proportion in sound and breath. Cosmos taught them to read the sky as a living text. It was never "math class." It was preparation for gnosis.

From this vantage, your yoga is not separate from the Quadrivium. It *is* the Quadrivium, embodied. Every time you count a ratio of breath, you are studying Number. Every time you inhabit a line of force in asana, you are practicing Geometry. Every time your nervous system entrains to mantra, you are learning Harmony. Every time you feel the difference between a new- moon practice and a full-moon practice, you are encountering Cosmos.

You realize that every Surya Namaskar has always been:

An arithmetic pattern. A geometric loop.

A piece of choreography in time.

A solar ritual inside a planetary field.

You are not adding the Quadrivium to your yoga.

You are finally seeing that your yoga has been the Quadrivium all along.

Number is how your balance feels from the inside. Geometry is how your bones remember alignment. Harmony is how your breath sings truth into your tissues.

Cosmos is how your nervous system orients itself in a universe that is not random. Cauda Pavonis is the stage where you stop privileging one of these over the others.

You no longer think of yourself as "a numbers

person," or "a body person," or "a sound person," or "a sky person."

You become a student of how all four are one teaching.

## Yoga as a Polyglot of Sacred Systems

Once the Quadrivium has stepped onto the stage, something else becomes obvious. Nothing you have studied has ever lived in isolation.

The bija mantra you chant is not just a sound. It is a syllable embedded in a web of letters, numbers, and planets.

The mudra you hold is not just a hand shape. It is a circuit connection that could be drawn as a diagram on the Archéomètre wheel.

The posture you enter is not just anatomy. It is a living glyph that could be read in Hebrew, Sanskrit, or Hermetic notation, if you knew how to see.

For most practitioners in the yoga world, the **Archéomètre** is an unknown word. Yet what it attempts to depict is very familiar to the part of you that has walked through Nigredo, Albedo, Citrinitas, and Rubedo. The Archéomètre, conceived by Saint-Yves d'Alveydre, is a great synthetic wheel—a map that lays out letters, sounds, colors, musical intervals, zodiacal signs, and sacred geometries as one coordinated field. It is not meant to replace any tradition; it is meant to show that all genuine traditions move across the same invisible grid.

Seen from this stage of your journey, the Archéomètre is less an abstract curiosity and more a mirror of what your nervous system is already doing. When you chant, move, breathe, and align, you are internally performing what the Archéomètre sketches externally: translating between sound, shape, number, and sky as a single act of consciousness.

Cauda Pavonis is the moment when systems like Kabbalah, Gematria, and the Archéomètre stop feeling like remote mysteries and start feeling like dictionaries for a language you already speak.

letter is a posture of sound.

Each number is a way consciousness organizes itself.

Each sign of the zodiac is a way the cosmos bends attention. Each planetary force is a way time thickens in your life.

You may not know the technical tables. You may never memorize correspondences. That is not the point. The point is that you begin to feel the principle behind them:

Reality is not random.

It is patterned in nested circles of twelve, seven, three, and one.

And your yoga practice has been slowly

initiating you into the ability to feel those patterns from the inside.

When you chant a simple OM and feel a resonance in the chest and skull, you are experiencing Harmony. When you realize that this OM could correspond to a Hebrew letter, a number, a color, and a position on a cosmic wheel, you are stepping into Number, Geometry, and Cosmos simultaneously.

The Archéomètre, in this light, is not just an esoteric apparatus. It is a picture of what happens when an awakened nervous system begins to perceive the one pattern that underlies alphabets, scales, colors, and cycles. It is a symbolic externalization of what Cauda Pavonis does internally.

Gematria, too, ceases to be playing with sacred arithmetic. It becomes a way of asking:

"If this word, this mantra, this Name equals this number, what is it telling me about the kind of movement of consciousness it carries into the world?"

In this stage, you don't need to leave yoga to "go study mysticism." Your practice becomes mysticism. You are the meeting place where Sanskrit seed syllables, Hebrew letters, planetary harmonics, and geometric postures converge.

You become the Peacock's Tail—

a single living spine displaying many languages at once.

## When Too Many Feathers Appear

There is a particular exhaustion that appears in Cauda Pavonis. It doesn't come from overwork. It comes from over-possibility.

You see too much. You recognize too many

connections. Every deity becomes an aspect of another deity. Every tradition feels secretly related. Every course, every training, every lineage seems to be offering a legitimate shard of the same whole.

If Rubedo tested you with intensity, Cauda Pavonis tests you with abundance.

There is a deep temptation here: to keep collecting colors instead of inhabiting them.

You may find yourself signing up for eight trainings at once, stacking certifications, sampling lineages, stitching together playlists of Sufi chants, Vedic mantras, Kirtan, Gregorian hymns, indigenous songs, and binaural beats. Your bookshelf multiplies. Your practice fragments into experiments.

You are not wrong to be drawn to all of this. The peacock's tail is meant to open.

But if you try to live in all of its eyes at once, you will exhaust yourself.

Cauda Pavonis is not asking you to become a spiritual tourist. It is teaching you that your consciousness is now capable of holding multiplicity without denying unity.

The task at this stage is not to choose which feather is "right." The task is to ask:

"What is the one light that all of these colors are trying to show me?" Which is another way of asking:

"What is the particular ray of this spectrum that I am here to embody?"

That question cannot be answered yet. It belongs to the next stage—Distillation. But Cauda Pavonis is where you first feel the tension between infinite options and singular vocation.

You stand in the middle of a kaleidoscope and realize you cannot walk in every direction at once. Something in you begins to whisper:

"It is time to know not only that all paths are one,

but which way this one body, this one life, must walk."

## The Nervous System in a Prism

If Rubedo was the test of whether your nervous system could conduct fire, Cauda Pavonis is the test of whether it can conduct variety without losing center.

On the mat, it looks like this:

One day your practice is fierce and martial. The next day it is soft and devotional. Another day it is geometric and precise. Another day it is mostly chanting. Yet through all of this, there is a new constant— an axis of awareness that does not swing with the mood.

You begin to notice that your system can move between qualities:

From linear to spiralic. From structured to fluid. From silent to sung.

From introspective to planetary. Without losing coherence.

This is the nervous-system signature of Cauda Pavonis:

You can change mode without changing essence.

Your breath can carry a Trataka stillness one moment and a Bhakti devotional the next, and yet the same witness remains. Asana can be expressed in Ashtanga rigor, Kundalini release, or Shakti spontaneous ecstatic flow, and yet the same geometry holds inside you. You begin to realize that styles are feathers— variations on a deeper pattern, not identities to defend.

At this point, the Quadrivium stops being an abstract set of four categories and becomes a diagnostic:

When you feel scattered, you check your Number:

Is there a clear count, a rhythm, a commitment to sequence?

When you feel disembodied, you check your Geometry:

Are you inhabiting bones, lines, spirals, points of contact with earth?

When you feel flat or mechanical, you check your Harmony:

Is there breath as music, sound, cadence, tone?

When you feel lost, you check your Cosmos:

Where are you in the day, in the moon, in the year, in the sky of your own psyche?

You have not left yoga.

You have entered yoga as a fourfold instrument of consciousness.

## The Multiplicity of Lineages in One Body

In earlier chapters we spoke of Kemetic solar alignments, Taoist standing postures, Vedic sun worship, shamanic trance, Hermetic breath, Indigenous ordeal.

Cauda Pavonis is where you begin to feel them not as separate histories, but as simultaneous presences in your own practice.

An Egyptian priest might recognize your spine in Urdhva Dhanurasana. A Taoist adept might recognize your breath in Nadi Shodhana.

A Kabbalist might recognize your chanting as

the descent of letters.

A Druid might recognize your walking meditation as tree-communion.

A Hermeticist might see your sequence as an operation of the four elements.

An astronomer might recognize your timing as resonant with a particular transit. You become, quite literally, a crossroads of traditions.

This is not appropriation. It is fulfillment of a human capacity: the ability of consciousness to host many streams of wisdom without confusing them, without flattening them, without needing to collapse them into sameness or hierarchy.

Cauda Pavonis does not say "all paths are identical." It says:

"All genuine paths rhyme in the deep structure of how they move consciousness from ignorance to coherence."

As someone walking this yoga, you become

able to hear that rhyme.

You see how a particular yama echoes a particular sephirah on the Tree of Life. How a certain asana echoes a certain card of the Tarot as an embodied archetype. How a breathing pattern mirrors a musical interval. How your own life cycle turns through zodiacal gates whether you believe in astrology or not.

You do not need to prove these things.

You only need to recognize that your soul is fluent in more languages than your education ever admitted.

## The First Glimpse of the Stone

Though the Philosopher's Stone is still ahead, Cauda Pavonis gives you your first true glimpse of what it will mean.

You begin to suspect that the Stone is not a substance, not an object, not a ritual artifact.

It is a consciousness capable of translating between Number, Geometry, Harmony, and Cosmos at will—a mind-body that can hear a mantra and see its geometry, feel its number, sense its planetary resonance, and understand its ethical implication all at once.

It is a human being who can move between yogic, Kabbalistic, Hermetic, Indigenous, scientific, and artistic vocabularies without losing their center, because they are no longer identified with any one expression.

The Stone is not a thing you will possess.

It is the name for what you are slowly becoming.

Cauda Pavonis is the stage where this becomes thinkable.

You feel, for the first time, that your work with yoga and alchemy and sacred geometry and numerology and cosmic timing is not a set of side-interests. It is a single curriculum preparing you for a specific vocation:

To be a bridge between worlds. Not as performance.

Not as branding.

But as a simple fact of what your nervous system will be able to hold, translate, and transmit. And yet, there is a problem.

You cannot live as the Stone while you are still in love with options. You cannot inhabit vocation while you are still sampling possibilities.

Which is why Cauda Pavonis is not the end. It is the expansion before the narrowing.

The spectrum before the single beam.

## The Quiet Thirst for Distillation

At first, Cauda Pavonis feels like arrival.

Everything you've studied begins to speak to everything else. Your mat becomes an altar of converging sciences. Your life events line up with transits, numbers, geometries, myths. You feel as if you are holding a kaleidoscope made of your own history.

But slowly, something inside begins to ache.

The ache is not for more information. It is for clarity of function. You begin to feel questions rising from a deeper place:

"With all that I now see, what am I here to actually do?"

"Which practices are essential for my path, and which are beautiful but non-essential?"

"What is my specific offering in this spectrum

of possibilities?"

"Where must my yoga, my fire, my Quadrivium, my inheritance actually land?"

You realize that if you continue only expanding, you will dissipate. If you continue only integrating, you will never embody. If you continue only collecting feathers, you will never fly.

The very multiplicity that thrilled you begins to demand a next step. Something in you whispers:

"It is time to boil this down. Not to make it smaller—

to make it potable, transmissible, usable,

for this one life, in this one body, for these people, in this time."

That impulse is not regression.

It is the call of the sixth stage of the Work.

Distillation.

## The Threshold

You stand now at the fifth gate of the alchemical journey. Behind you:

Blackness undone.

Whitening of breath. Dawning gold of structure. Red fire of will.

An opened tail of iridescent connections.

Ahead of you:

The still, hot work of choosing what remains.

The careful boiling-down of a thousand colors into a handful of medicines.

The transformation of your vast inner curriculum into a path that can actually be walked—by you and by those who will one day walk with you.

Cauda Pavonis has shown you the richness of the field. Distillation will ask:

"What of this richness must become your daily vow?" And beyond that, at the far horizon, waits the Stone—

the integration of yoga, alchemy, Quadrivium, Archéomètre, numerology, and cosmic geometry

into a single, embodied human presence.

But before the Stone can harden, before the final seal can be set,

the Work must pass through the alembic once more.

Everything you have gathered must now be refined. And so we turn, in the next chapter,

from the brightness of the Peacock's Tail

to the quiet, relentless clarity of **Distillation**.

CHAPTER SIX

# DISTILLATIO

*The Narrowing· The Choosing· The Making of the Essential*

*"Not everything that is true must be carried forward. Some truths arrive only to teach us what we are ready to release."*

— ***Tracy Shearer***

*"I discovered that clarity is not expansion—it is courage. It is the willingness to let a thousand lights fall away so that one steady flame can finally speak."*

— ***Dr. Enolia Harris Pedro***

## *Boiling Down the Infinite · The Alembic of Vocation*

By the time you arrive here, abundance is no longer theory. You have felt it in your bones.

Nigredo emptied you. Albedo rinsed you.

Citrinitas gave you structure. Rubedo set you on fire.

Cauda Pavonis opened a hundred doors at once.

You have tasted many paths, many systems, many languages of the sacred. Your mat has become a crossroads. Your bookshelf a convergence of worlds. Your nervous system, a prism.

For a while, this is exhilarating. Then—quietly—it becomes unsustainable.

There comes a morning when you roll out your

mat and realize:

You could practice a dozen different ways today, and all of them are "right," but not all of them are *necessary.*

There comes a season when yet another training, yet another lineage, yet another powerful practice no longer feels like expansion. It feels like dilution.

Cauda Pavonis showed you the spectrum. Distillatio asks:

"What of this must now become *essence*?"

Distillation in the laboratory is simple and ruthless. Heat is applied. The mixture boils. Vapors rise, condense, and are collected. What is coarse remains at the bottom. What is volatile leaves. What is precious is gathered as a clear, concentrated liquid. Distillation in yoga is no different.

Your life becomes the alembic.

Your daily rhythm becomes the flame.

Your practices become the mixture.

Your attention becomes the collector.

What cannot survive repeated passes of heat and clarity falls away. What remains, drop by drop, is your *vocation*.

## The Weariness of "More"

The first sign of Distillatio is not ecstasy. It is weariness.

Not the weariness of burnout, but the weariness of someone who has eaten a magnificent feast and realizes they cannot take another bite.

You notice it in small ways.

The endless menu of workshops and trainings no longer excites you. Endless playlists and practices begin to blur into sameness.

More information does not comfort. It crowds.

You feel a subtle nausea toward spiritual consumption. This is not cynicism. It is saturation.

The nervous system has reached a threshold. It has proven that it can:

Endure blackness without disintegrating.
Circulate sensation without drowning.

Perceive geometry without clinging to form.
Conduct fire without burning itself.

Hold multiplicity without fragmenting. Now it turns toward a different hunger:

"Enough. Show me what is *mine*." You begin to ask, almost in a whisper:

"With all that I can now see and do... what actually matters for this life?"

The industry around you still chants "more": more certifications, more modalities, more offerings, more platforms, more tools.

Distillatio answers with a different mantra:

"Less, but truer."

## Heat Without Novelty

In earlier stages, heat brought novelty. New sensations. New insights. New capacity. In Distillatio, the heat returns—but without the reward of constant 'newness.'

You may find yourself repeating the same sequence day after day, the same mantra, the same pranayama ratio, the same silent sitting. At first, the ego resists: *This is boring. I need variation. I need to grow.*

But distillation does not care about entertainment. It cares about *clarity*.

A simple morning practice, done relentlessly, becomes a still-point around which all the brilliance of Cauda Pavonis is slowly boiled down. One mantra begins to gather ten mantras inside it. One sequence begins to summarize ten trainings. One altar begins to stand for a hundred temples.

Your ego complains. Your soul exhales.

Because finally, there is less to manage. Less to remember.

Less to prove.

What remains is what you would do even if no one were watching.

What remains is what you would still practice if

every outer structure of yoga vanished. What remains is what you cannot *not* do.

Distillation is the stage where you discover which practices are truly non-negotiable—and which were beautiful, powerful, genuine, but ultimately preparatory.

## The Quadrivium in the Alembic

At Cauda Pavonis, the Quadrivium stepped forward as four simultaneous languages of your yoga: Number, Geometry, Harmony, Cosmos.

In Distillatio, you begin to refine how each of these will live in *your* path. Not as four separate disciplines, but as four facets of a single vow.

Number is distilled into specific rhythms and counts that truly sustain you. You may have experimented with dozens of pranayama ratios, mala counts, cycle structures. Now, a few reveal

themselves as essential. Perhaps it is a simple 4–7–8 breath that calms your system so deeply you feel your whole life reorganize. Perhaps it is the 108-bead journey of one mantra that cuts through every mental storm. You stop chasing rarefied numbers and begin honoring the few that your body recognizes as home.

Geometry, too, is distilled. You no longer need a vast catalogue of postures to feel complete. You see, with sudden clarity, that there are certain shapes your soul came here to inhabit: the verticality of Tree, the arcs of backbends, the triangular intelligence of standing poses, the spirals of twists. Other asanas become allies, but not centerpieces. Your personal mandala narrows. The body says, "These are the forms through which my dharma speaks."

Harmony distills into a recognizable voice. You may have chanted in many languages, sung many mantras, explored many tonalities. Yet a handful of sounds now ring uniquely true in your bones. A seed syllable, a simple OM, a particular name of the Divine, a wordless hum, a melody that seems to open your chest every time—it is these that remain when the rest are gently allowed to fade. Your nervous system no longer wants a global playlist. It wants a clear tuning fork.

Cosmos is distilled into a few chosen alignments. No one can consciously track every transit, every eclipse, every astrological nuance. Distillatio asks: which cosmic rhythms genuinely shape the way you live and practice? Maybe you commit to respecting the lunar cycle—new moon for emptiness, full moon for offering. Maybe you honor solstices and equinoxes, or sunrise and sunset as two unshakable daily anchors. You stop pretending you will "follow everything." You choose a few celestial gates and build your days around them.

The Quadrivium does not disappear here. It becomes *personal.*

Number, Geometry, Harmony, and Cosmos condense into a handful of lived commitments that no longer feel like study. They feel like *being yourself on purpose.*

## The Archéomètre in Miniature

On the scale of civilizations, the Archéomètre is an immense universal wheel—colors, notes, letters, zodiac, geometries, all mapped as one coherent mandala.

On the scale of a human life in Distillatio, the Archéomètre shrinks. It moves from diagram to nervous system.

You no longer need to hold the whole wheel in mind. Instead, you begin to feel that your particular path lights up only a few of its segments, again and again.

Perhaps there is a specific spectrum of color

that keeps returning in your visions and clothes and altars, a set of tones your voice loves, a handful of letters or names you are drawn to, a small portion of the zodiac you continually work through. Distillation invites you to recognize: *this is my slice of the wheel.*

You are not meant to embody every correspondence.

You are meant to embody the ones that form your signature.

In this way, yoga, alchemy, Quadrivium, and Archéomètre stop being huge architectures outside you. They become a small number of precise resonances that your body, heart, and voice keep repeating across years.

Over time, this repetition builds a recognizable field around you. People will not say, "She knows every system."

They will say, "She carries something very specific, and I feel it whenever I'm near her." That specificity is Distillatio completing its work.

## Saying No as Sacred Heat

In earlier stages, sacred heat mostly appeared *on* the mat: in long holds, in challenging postures, in breath suspensions, in the ache of Rubedo, the blazing abundance of Cauda Pavonis.

In Distillatio, the fiercest heat lives in a much simpler place:

In your ability to say "no".

No to the training that pulls you toward dispersion rather than destiny. No to the collaboration that dilutes the core of your work.

No to the lifestyle that erodes your practice.

No to the teaching opportunities that ask you to perform a version of yourself you have already outgrown.

Each "no" is a tiny act of distillation.

Each "no" boils off a layer of the unnecessary.

The alchemy here is subtle and brutal.

You realize that you can no longer afford to spend your fire in directions that do not serve your vow. Not because you have become rigid, but because you have become *finite* to yourself. You feel the actual limits of your body, your days, your years. You sense that there is a precise quantum of life-force available to you in this incarnation, and you are no longer willing to squander it on what is almost-right.

Distillatio turns boundaries into a sacrament.

Not walls against the world—

but channels that conserve and direct your stream.

## When Practice Begins to Distill You

For many in the yoga world, this is also the stage where teaching or practicing stops being only an expression and begins to act back upon you as a refining fire.

You watch yourself in the role of practitioner or teacher to see, with increasing clarity: Which words are real, and which are filler.

Which cues are transmission, and which are habit.

Which stories still carry charge, and which are old identity trying to survive.

You notice how often you reach for complexity when a simple instruction would do. You notice when you are performing a lineage instead of serving the people in front of you. You notice how certain classes leave you nourished and others drain you, not because of the participants, but because of the posture you took inside yourself.

Distillatio asks you, again and again:

"What is the simplest, truest thing I can offer here that is actually mine to give?" Everything else is allowed to evaporate.

Your classes may become simpler on the surface—less choreography, fewer themes, more space. But for those who can feel, the potency intensifies. The signal-to-noise ratio shifts. The practice becomes clean. Even if you use many elements—asana, mantra, philosophy, ritual—there is now a clear center that holds.

Practicing or teaching, in this way, stops being a performance of knowledge and becomes a daily still opened by fire. You pour yourself in, meet your own edges, and emerge a little clearer each time.

## Refining Desire

One of the most delicate operations of Distillatio is the refinement of desire.

In earlier stages, desire was information: it revealed where you were stuck, where you were hungry, where you yearned, where you feared. In Rubedo, desire became combustible—fuel for action, creation, devotion. In Cauda Pavonis, desire multiplied, stretching toward many beauties at once.

Here, desire becomes a field that must be clarified.

You begin to see that some desires are simply old patterns wearing new costumes. Some are reactions to the industry's narratives of success. Some are survival strategies dressed up as spiritual callings. Some are genuine, but belong to earlier versions of you.

Distillatio warms this entire field until the

transient vapors of false or secondary desires lift away.

What remains are a few deep currents that do not fluctuate with mood or trend. A desire to serve a certain kind of person or community.

A desire to protect or restore something in the world.

A desire to explore a particular question all the way down.

A desire to build a very specific bridge between traditions, disciplines, or worlds. These do not shout. They hum.

They have been humming since before you knew the language of yoga, and they will continue humming after your role as "yoga practitioner" or "yoga teacher" has dissolved. They are not owned by the industry. They are the contours of your soul's assignment.

Distillatio teaches you to recognize these fundamental desires and distinguish them from both passing cravings and abstract ideals. The moment you do, your practice reorganizes itself around them.

## Life as the Final Sequence

At this stage, practice and life begin to exchange roles. Earlier, you practiced on the mat to prepare for life.

Now, you live in such a way that your whole life becomes the final, distilled sequence.

You notice that the same principles you use to structure a class now shape your days: A clear opening.

A build of heat.

A peak of effort.

A conscious release. An intentional closing.

You begin to hold your year as a mandala: seasons of intensity, seasons of repose, days for outward teaching, days for inward study. You are no longer content to drop your Quadrivium perception when you step out of the studio or off the mat. Number, Geometry,

Harmony, and Cosmos follow you into your scheduling, your finances, your relationships.

A conversation becomes an asana.

A difficult decision becomes pranayama.

A grief cycle becomes Surya Namaskar.

A new project becomes a mantra taken up for a season.

Distillation is the point where "yoga" ceases to be a distinguishable activity and becomes the way you do everything.

You are not practicing to accumulate experiences anymore.

You are practicing to maintain a **state** from which your assignment can be carried out with as little distortion as possible.

## The Slow Realization: This Is My Ray

Over months and years of Distillatio, something dawns so softly you might almost miss it. You notice that people come to you for the same kinds of things.

You notice that certain teachings keep returning in your classes, even when you try to change

them.

You notice that your body keeps arranging postures in familiar arcs.

You notice that your own crises keep circling around a few central themes, each time yielding deeper insight.

You realize:

"I have a ray."

Not a brand. Not a niche. Not a persona.

A ray of the one light that it seems you were born to carry.

Perhaps your ray is fierce clarity. Perhaps it is tender restoration.

Perhaps it is bridging worlds—science and mysticism, therapy and ritual, elders and youth, North and South, East and West.

Perhaps it is sound. Perhaps it is silence.

Perhaps it is bodies remembering they are geometry, or hearts remembering they are altars, or communities remembering they are mandalas.

Whatever it is, it repeats.

Distillation is the stage where you stop resisting that repetition and begin to *honor* it. The practices, systems, and languages that truly serve this ray remain.

The rest is released with gratitude.

You are no longer trying to be everything.

You are becoming precisely what you came here to be.

## The Doorway to the Stone

Distillatio is not as spectacular as Rubedo. There are fewer visions than in Cauda Pavonis, fewer dramatic releases than in Nigredo, fewer obvious breakthroughs than in Albedo and Citrinitas.

From the outside, it can look like someone quietly simplifying their life. From the inside, it is the most exacting work of all.

Because here you are not only transforming. You are choosing.

You are choosing which aspects of the Quadrivium will define your vows.

You are choosing which correspondences of the Archéomètre truly belong to your line of work. You are choosing which inheritances from Kemetic, Vedic, Taoist, Hermetic,

Indigenous, and modern lineages you will carry forward—and which you will reverently set down.

Every choice is a cut. Every cut is an offering. Every offering clears the way for the final integration. Beyond Distillatio waits the seventh gate:

The Stone.

Not as mystery object or legendary artifact, but as the name for a consciousness in which yoga, alchemy, Quadrivium, Archéomètre, numerology, and cosmic geometry have ceased to be separate conversations and have become **one lived reality**.

You are not there yet. You are condensing.

Drop by drop. Practice by practice. Yes by yes. No by no.

Until one day, without spectacle, the Work inside you is no longer a process. It is a presence.

And when that presence stabilizes,

the Philosopher's Stone is no longer a legend on the page. It is the way you walk into a room.

In the next chapter, we will finally speak its name.

## CHAPTER SEVEN

# THE PHILOSOPHER'S STONE

*Coherence · Transmission · The Living Seal*

*"The moment is not when light is found—but when you become trustworthy enough to carry it without distortion."*

— ***Tracy Shearer***

*"The moment I could no longer separate Number from action, Geometry from ethics, Music from speech, or Cosmos from responsibility—I knew the Quadrivium had completed its work in me."*

— ***Dr. Enolia Harris Pedro***

## *The Human as Completed Instrument · The Integration of All Arts into One Presence*

There is no dramatic moment when the Stone announces itself. No thunder.

No public coronation.

No final posture that proves completion.

If anything, its arrival is quieter than all that came before.

Because the Philosopher's Stone is not an object you acquire. It is not a secret you decode.

It is not a title you earn.

It is the moment when there is no longer anything in you that is *outside* the Work.

Nigredo, Albedo, Citrinitas, Rubedo, Cauda Pavonis, Distillatio—each of these reshaped something fundamental in your relationship to form, sensation, pattern, will, multiplicity, and choice. Each was a refinement. Each was a burning-away.

The Stone is what remains **when nothing is left that needs to be transformed**. Not because you are perfect.

But because you are no longer divided.

The oppositions that once fought inside you—mind versus body, mysticism versus discipline, devotion versus clarity, action versus contemplation, science versus spirit—no longer need mediation.

They have become one language.

The Stone is not the end of practice. It is the end of fragmentation.

## What the Stone Actually Is

In old texts, the Philosopher's Stone is

described through a cascade of images that seem, at first glance, to contradict one another:

A red stone.

A white powder. A tincture.

A crystal.

A medicine.

A spark of divine fire trapped in matter.

A solvent that dissolves everything and leaves only gold.

To the uninitiated, these appear like poetic excess or symbolic confusion. But to those who have traveled the full arc of the Work, these images are not contradictions at all. They are different ways of describing the same phenomenon as it reveals itself through different layers of reality.

The Stone looks red when it moves through

blood and will. It looks white when it purifies perception.

It becomes tincture when it infuses life invisibly. It appears as crystal when it stabilizes structure. It becomes medicine when it restores coherence. It feels like fire when it ignites purpose.

It behaves like solvent when it dissolves what is false. And it leaves gold when only truth remains.

These are not stages of acquiring something new.

They are stages of **what remains when distortion has been removed**. The Stone is not an object that is added to the human being.

It is what the human being becomes

after everything that interferes with coherence has been burned away. And this is the key that most interpretations miss:

The Stone is coherence that survives in matter.

Not coherence in theory. Not coherence in belief.

Not coherence in philosophy. But coherence in:

Breath — where life enters and leaves without resistance. Posture — where gravity and will collaborate instead of compete. Speech — where truth moves without violence or concealment.

Decision — where choice arises without fragmentation. Time use — where urgency and patience no longer battle. Relationship — where intimacy does not require erasure.

Creation — where what is made carries the signature of alignment. Silence — where nothing needs to be defended.

This is the slow, hidden journey of the Great Work:

from fragmentation into coherence, from interference into transparency, from distortion into resonance.

The Stone is the moment when the human instrument becomes so internally aligned

that **whatever passes through it–knowledge, emotion, sound, geometry, number, timing–emerges without distortion**. Nothing is rejected. Nothing is dramatized. Nothing is possessed. Everything is conducted.

This is why the Stone was never owned by rulers, priests, or institutions for long. Because coherence cannot be standardized.

It cannot be legislated.

It cannot be mass-produced.

It cannot be preserved by hierarchy.

It dissolves the very structures that try to trap it.

The Stone has always terrified power built on distortion, because it exposes without attacking and reorganizes without overthrowing. It cannot be weaponized without ceasing to be what it is.

It could not be contained by structure. It could only live in a person.

And that is why yoga, in its deepest sense, has always been a preparation for the Stone—whether it named it or not.

## The Stone as the Living Quadrivium

At last, the Quadrivium ceases to be a framework you "apply." It becomes **how you exist**.

Number is no longer something you calculate.

It is how your actions fall into exact measure without strain.

Your "yes" arrives when it must. Your "no" lands cleanly.

Your rest occurs when cycles close.

Your effort rises when pressure is required.

You no longer rush ahead of time. You no longer lag behind it.

Number now lives as **right timing**.

Geometry is no longer something you visualize.

It is how your body organizes itself in space without correction.

You stand where you must stand.

You withdraw when lines of force demand withdrawal. You turn when vectors shift.

Your posture in life becomes as precise as your posture on the mat ever was. Harmony is no longer something you create with chanting alone.

It is how your voice, your breath, your tone, your pacing, your listening naturally entrain others.

People feel regulated in your presence. Not because you try to heal them—

but because your nervous system has become a tuning fork for coherence.

Cosmos is no longer something you track through charts or ephemerides.

It is how your life arranges itself in synchrony with larger movements you no longer need to define.

You feel when to plant. When to withdraw.

When to speak publicly. When to disappear into study. When to wait.

When to act.

The sky now moves inside your blood without names. This is what it means to *be* the Quadrivium.

## The Archéomètre No Longer Outside You

At earlier stages, the Archéomètre appeared as a grand map of correspondences—letters, tones, colors, planets, numbers, signs.

At the stage of the Stone, that wheel collapses inward. You no longer consult it.

**You are arranged like it**.

Your voice carries tonal intelligence without effort. Your words land with numerical precision.

Your movements trace geometry without conscious planning. Your timing obeys cycles without conscious tracking.

Hebrew letters, Sanskrit vibrations, Hermetic ratios, Kemetic solar arcs—these no longer appear as separate systems.

They appear as **one current of intelligence**

**moving through different historical mouths.** You stop translating between systems.

They translate themselves through you.

## What the Stone Does to Identity

This is the part that most books avoid saying clearly: The Stone dissolves identity without erasing personality.

You still have preferences. You still have style.

You still have temperament.

But you no longer confuse these with authorship. You no longer say:

"This is my teaching." "This is my power." "This is my knowledge." "This is my path."

You say, inwardly: "I am being used."

Not as submission. As accuracy.

Because nothing in you feels owned by ego anymore.

Your abilities feel borrowed.

Your insights feel forwarded rather than produced. Your influence feels entrusted rather than seized.

This is why the Stone has always terrified empires. It cannot be branded.

It cannot be centralized.

It cannot be reproduced on demand.

It moves wherever coherence finds a human vessel capable of holding it.

## The Stone as the End of Seeking

The most obvious sign that the Stone has stabilized is simple: You stop hunting experiences.

You stop asking, "What's next?"

You stop trying to upgrade your awakening.

You stop measuring yourself against anyone

else's realization.

Not because you have become complacent—but because seeking has fulfilled its purpose.

Nothing inside you is still trying to *become*. What remains is commitment to functioning. Your question is no longer:

"How do I grow?"

Your question becomes:

"How do I serve what has grown in me?" This does not remove difficulty.

It removes noise.

Life will still pressure you. Loss will still come.

Illness will still visit. Conflict will still arise.

But none of it destabilizes your center anymore. You break—and remain whole.

## The Stone and the World

The Stone has never belonged to monasteries alone. The Stone is not optimized for withdrawal.

It is optimized for **impact without distortion**.

When the Stone stabilizes, your life becomes catalytic whether you intend it or not. Children feel seen in your presence.

Strangers tell you truths they didn't know they carried. Groups reorganize unconsciously.

Systems shift when you enter them.

Not because you dominate.

But because coherence forces re-alignment.
The Stone does not save the world.

It changes what the world can no longer hide.

This is why those who carry it are often misunderstood. Misnamed.

Projected onto. Idealized.

Attacked.

The Stone neutralizes false structures simply by existing inside them.

Yoga as the Preparation for the Stone

This is the full arc of what you have actually been doing in yoga all along—whether anyone ever named it for you or not.

You began with the body because matter must be addressed first. You cleared stagnation.

You learned circulation. You awakened structure. You survived ignition.

You held multiplicity. You chose essence.

Now the body is no longer obstacle or instrument alone. It is the **vessel of the Stone**.

Your spine becomes the vertical axis of transmission. Your breath becomes the regulator of subtle fire.

Your heart becomes the furnace that does not crack.

Your voice becomes the conductor of truth without violence. Your hands become the geometry of service.

Your feet become timing.

Asana becomes effortless accuracy.
Pranayama becomes silent command.
Meditation becomes unbroken presence.
Mantra becomes the hum of living structure.

Yoga no longer feels like a practice you do. It feels like the way your existence operates.

## The Final Secret

There is one last truth the alchemists hid inside riddles because it cannot be taught without being misunderstood:

The Stone does not make you extraordinary. It makes you **ordinary without illusion**.

You still cook. You still wash.

You still make mistakes. You still love imperfectly. You still grieve.

But none of these contradict the Work anymore. They are the Work.

Gold is not something you add to life.

Gold is what life becomes when nothing falsifies it.

## The End of the Book, the Beginning of the Stone

This book ends here not because the journey is finished—

but because the journey has become indistinguishable from living. The Seven Stages were never ladders.

They were a description of how consciousness learns to survive in matter without lying to itself. You now carry:

The dissolution that can face darkness.

The circulation that can feel without drowning. The structure that can see without freezing.

The fire that can act without corrupting.

The spectrum that can hold many paths without confusion. The essence that can choose without contraction.

And now—

The Stone that can remain coherent in the middle of the world. Nothing beyond this needs explanation.

Because from here forward, explanation becomes example. You do not teach the Stone.

You walk it into rooms.

And those who are ready will recognize it— not by brilliance,

but by the sudden feeling, in their own bodies, that something in them has finally become possible.

## Tracy Shearer

Tracy Shearer is a Board-Certified Holistic Health Practitioner through the American Association of Drugless Practitioners (AADP), a Certified Holistic Nutrition, Health, and Wellness Coach, and a graduate of the T. Colin Campbell Foundation Plant-Based Nutrition certification program at Cornell University. Her work stands at the powerful intersection of nutrition, movement, and conscious lifestyle design.

Tracy has over 30 years of professional, award-winning experience in process re-engineering, change management, and organizational administration. She has held several leadership, managerial, and directorship roles across a wide range of industries, including municipalities, education, and business process outsourcing both domestically and internationally. Her work focused on building efficient, accountable systems and processes while guiding corporations, organizations and individuals through complex shifts with clarity and purpose while supporting sustainable transition through strategic and holistic perspectives.

Tracy is a graduate of the yoga teacher training programs at both The Kaivalya Yoga Method Academy and the Yogamu Institute Teaching Academy. She holds the distinction of being a 500- hour Registered Yoga Teacher (RYT-500) with Yoga Alliance, a 200-hour Certified Meditation Teacher with Meditation Alliance International, and a 100-hour Certified Kundalini Teacher. She is also a founding member of the Global Yoga Therapy and Ayurveda Organization (GYTA), where she continues to contribute to the advancement of therapeutic yoga worldwide.

In addition, Tracy is a Certified Empower

Achieve Succeed (EAS) Self-Mastery Coach and a recognized Certified Practitioner with the Complementary Therapists Accredited Association, serving clients internationally across the United States, Canada, Europe, and Africa.

Through her global wellness platform, **Flourish With Tracy**, she is devoted to empowering individuals to cultivate sustainable self-care practices—helping people *eat better, move better, and live better*. Her work blends modern science with ancient wisdom, always guided by compassion, embodiment, and practical transformation.

**Website:** https://www.flourishwithtracy.com/

# Dr. Enolia Harris Pedro

Dr. Enolia Harris Pedro is a scholar, global educator, author, award-winning speaker, business executive, and ceremonial elder whose work bridges classical philosophy, sacred geometry, consciousness studies, and applied pedagogy. Her teaching and writing are grounded in the conviction that true education is not the accumulation of information, but the disciplined formation of the intellect toward truth, coherence, and wisdom.

An initiated and formally recognized **Grandmother Elder and Medicine Woman of the Ojibwe**, Dr. Harris Pedro has studied with Indigenous elders and knowledge keepers from the Ojibwe, Lakota, Yaqui, Hopi, and Apache Nations of North America; the Mapuche of Chile; the Toltec of Mexico; the

Waitaha of Aotearoa (New Zealand); and the Luhya of Kenya. Honored as an Indigenous Matriarch and Elder, she guides, heals, and mentors communities and leaders worldwide, preserving and transmitting ancient cosmological lineages while supporting contemporary leadership and social transformation.

She has also been initiated and formally acknowledged within the cosmological traditions of the **Q'ero People of Peru** and within the **Ovimbundu traditions of Africa**. Guided by teachings received from elders across Africa, the Americas, and other ancestral lineages, she has spent decades examining how worth is constructed, disrupted, and restored across cultures. Her work integrates sacred geometry, cosmology, embodied knowledge, and lived pedagogy—grounded not in abstraction, but in coherence, relational intelligence, and daily practice.

An internationally recognized, award-winning speaker, Dr. Harris Pedro has addressed audiences around the world—youth and adults alike—on self-mastery, conscious coherence, and navigating what she terms the *innerverse* of human experience. Her writing journey began with short stories published in various magazines and evolved into a comprehensive body of work focused on personal development, intellectual formation, ethical consciousness, and mastery-based learning.

Trained through both formal study and traditional mentorship, Dr. Harris Pedro's scholarship is deeply informed by the classical liberal arts tradition—particularly the **Trivium and Quadrivium**—as well as **Platonic, Aristotelian, and Thomistic philosophy**. Her engagement with these foundations is paired with decades of experience in teaching, facilitation, and curriculum development across interdisciplinary and cross-cultural contexts.

She holds a **Bachelor of Science in Mathematics** from the University of Massachusetts Amherst and an **MBA from Regis University**, where she graduated *summa* *cum laude* and was inducted into the **Alpha Sigma Nu Honor Society**. She also holds a **Doctorate in International Peace** (United Nations) and a **Doctorate of Humanities** (United Nature International Peace Organization).

Dr. Harris Pedro is the founder and principal of **ENOLIA International LLC**, a publishing, education, and media company dedicated to restoring depth, rigor, and integrity to modern learning. Through ENOLIA International and its associated platforms, she has developed mastery-based programs, broadcasts, and written works exploring self-mastery, sacred geometry, cosmology, and the ethical formation of consciousness. She is also a founding voice behind **Wombology**, a global media platform amplifying culturally and spiritually grounded perspectives across more than forty countries.

In addition to her writing and teaching, Dr. Harris Pedro hosts the podcast ***The Infinite Way - Where Spirituality Meets Humanity***, available on YouTube. Through this platform, she engages scholars, practitioners, and thought leaders in conversations exploring the meeting point of spirituality, philosophy, lived experience, and contemporary human challenges. The podcast serves as an extension of her pedagogical mission—bringing depth, discernment, and coherence to modern discourse while honoring timeless wisdom traditions.

She is the author of numerous works, including *Sacred Geometry in Motion: From Number to Cosmic Consciousness*; *The Alchemical Path of Yoga: Seven Stages to Living Coherence*; *The Quadrivium*; *The Sovereignty of Worth: Conscious Coherence and the True Self*; *Know Thyself: A 30-Day Program to Conscious Living*; *The Seven Principles for Self-Mastery: The Empower, Achieve, Succeed Methodology*; *Finding My Sovereign Voice with My Grandmother Elder*; and *Discover Your Sovereign Self Journal*. She is also the creator of the **Empower, Achieve, Succeed Through Self-Mastery (EAS)** methodology—an integrated framework for personal, intellectual, and ethical development used in coaching and educational settings.

Her approach to teaching has been shaped by early mentorship under elders and advanced scholars, including foundational mastery-level study within the **LaserEduLogics** framework. These formative experiences cultivated a lifelong commitment to apprenticeship, precision in language, and deep respect for the lineage and transmission of knowledge.

In addition to her academic and media work, Dr. Harris Pedro leads **immersive retreats and educational expeditions** designed for deep personal, intellectual, and spiritual development. These offerings provide sustained study, ceremonial practice, and reflective inquiry, allowing participants to engage wisdom traditions as lived experience rather than abstraction. Her retreats and expeditions span the **Americas, Africa, Europe, Australia, India, and Asia**, integrating classical learning, indigenous knowledge, and contemporary self-mastery within culturally grounded and ethically guided settings.

*The Trivium: Ancient Wisdom for Modern Times* represents Dr. Harris Pedro's most comprehensive pedagogical work to date. Drawing deeply from **Sister Miriam Joseph's *The Trivium* (1947)**, this book serves as both a scholarly companion and a modern guide—designed to help contemporary students and instructors reclaim the intellectual architecture necessary for higher learning and contemplative mastery.

Dr. Harris Pedro continues to teach, write, and develop educational frameworks that honor the past while preparing the intellect for the demands of the present. Her work stands at the intersection of tradition and transformation, offering readers a path from knowledge to wisdom through disciplined study and lived understanding. Learn more about Dr. Enolia Harris Pedro at https://enolia.live.

# ALCHEMICAL & HERMETIC TERMINOLOGY

## Alchemy

A trans-civilizational sacred science originating in Kemet (Egypt), transmitted through the Hellenistic world, the Arabic Golden Age, India, China, and medieval Europe. Alchemy is the **science of transmutation**, not merely of metals but of consciousness through matter. It

encodes the universal law that fixed structures must dissolve, reorganize, and stabilize at higher coherence.

**Further Study:** Hermes Trismegistus, Zosimos of Panopolis, Paracelsus, Jung (*Psychology and Alchemy*).

## Nigredo (Blackening)

The first stage of the Magnum Opus. Symbolizes psychological, existential, and energetic dissolution. Associated with Saturn, decay, shadow emergence, and identity collapse. In this text, Nigredo is treated as **the Void of Emptiness**—the pre-structural field prior to reconstitution.

**Further Study:** Dark Night of the Soul (St. John of the Cross), Jungian shadow work.

## Albedo (Whitening)

The stage of purification and circulation following collapse. Connected with lunar symbolism, breath regulation, nervous system recalibration, parasympathetic coherence, and emotional clarity.

**Further Study:** Sacred washing rites, vagal tone research, pranayama science.

## Citrinitas (Yellowing / Dawning Gold)

The stage of emerging intelligibility where **pattern, number, and geometry become perceptible inside perception itself**. Often removed in later Western texts but foundational in Hermetic, Arabic, and Kemetic streams.

**Further Study**: Pythagorean number theory, Platonic geometry, Sol–gold correspondences.

## Rubedo (Reddening)

The stage of embodied fire, blood ignition, and ethical consequence. Transformation

becomes **irreversible**. Will, sexuality, voice, and heart coherence become operational powers.

**Further Study**: Tapas in yoga, Vedic Agni ritual, heart coherence science.

## Cauda Pavonis (Peacock's Tail)

The iridescent multicolored stage following unification. Consciousness can now

hold **multiplicity without fragmentation**. All traditions, systems, and symbols become perceivable as one light through many colors.

**Further Study:** Integral theory, syncretic mysticism, non-linear cognition.

## Distillation

The boiling down of multiplicity into essential function. Represents **vocation crystallization**, service refinement, and transmissible coherence.

**Further Study:** Alembic symbolism, contemplative minimalism, vocational psychology.

## Philosopher's Stone (Lapis Philosophorum)

The final stabilized coherence in matter. The Stone is **not an object but a state of embodied universal intelligence**, capable of transmitting pattern without distortion.

**Further Study:** Paracelsus, Jung's *Self Archetype*, Solar Body traditions.

## Solve et Coagula

Alchemical axiom meaning "dissolve and bind." The universal cycle of disintegration and reintegration at increasingly refined levels of order.

**Further Study:** Entropy/negentropy, systems theory.

## Mercurius

volatile intermediary principle of transformation—simultaneously fixed and fluid. Governs nervous system plasticity, breath, cognition, and psychopompic transitions.

**Further Study**: Planetary alchemy, Hermes mythology.

# YOGIC AND VEDIC SCIENCE TERMINOLOGY

## Yoga (योग)

From *yuj*, meaning to yoke or unite. Yoga is a **complete operational science of human coherence** integrating breath, posture, sound, ethics, and cosmic alignment.

**Further Study**: Patanjali, Tantra Yoga, Kashmir Shaivism.

## Asana (आसन)

A posture of psycho-physical stabilization serving as **living geometry for nervous system coherence**.

**Further Study**: Biotensegrity, myofascial chains.

### Prāṇāyāma (▮◌ाण◌ाय◌ाम)

The governance of life force through breath. The only system that bridges voluntary and involuntary neurological control.

**Further Study:** Respiratory neurophysiology.

### Prāṇa

The animating life-force underlying respiration, metabolism, cognition, and electromagnetic vitality.

**Further Study:** Biofield science, biophoton research.

### Five Vāyus (Pañca Vāyu)

Directional currents governing all movement in body and psyche:

- Prāṇa – intake

- Apāna – elimination
- Samāna – assimilation
- Udāna – ascent
- Vyāna – integration

**Further Study:** Autonomic nervous system mapping.

## Bandha

Neuromuscular pressure locks redirecting prāṇa through spinal channels.
**Further Study:** Pelvic neurology.

## Dṛṣṭi

Gaze fixation stabilizing optic–vestibular integration.
**Further Study:** Neuro-ocular motor research.

## Mudrā

Hand seals completing psychophysiological circuits.
**Further Study**: Cortical homunculus mapping.

### Tapas

Transformational heat generated through sustained discipline.
**Further Study**: Hormetic stress science.

### Kundalini

Latent spinal neuro-energetic intelligence governing ascension of consciousness.

**Further Study**: Cerebrospinal fluid and pineal dynamics.

**Further Study in Yoga, Holistic Wellness & Embodied Self-Mastery**

Readers wishing to deepen their **practical, therapeutic, nutritional, energetic, and integrative study of yoga as a living path** are encouraged to continue directly through the work of **Tracy Shearer**, whose platform offers applied transmission of the principles contained in this book.

Through **Flourish With Tracy**, students may engage in:

- Holistic Health & Wellness Coaching
- Yoga & Meditation Instruction
- Kundalini & Energetic Integration
- Plant-Based Nutrition for Vibrational Health
- Empower Achieve Succeed (EAS) Self-Mastery Training
- Lifestyle Coherence & Embodied Transformation
- Yoga Immersion and Teacher Certification Training

This platform serves as a **living laboratory of embodied yogic coherence** for modern life.

https://www.flourishwithtracy.com/

— *Tracy Shearer*

# THE QUADRIVIUM

## The Quadrivium – Definition, Origin, and Function

The **Quadrivium** is the classical fourfold science of reality:

- **Number (Arithmetic)** – vibration understood discretely
- **Geometry** – form in space
- **Harmony (Music)** – ratio in vibration
- **Cosmos (Astronomy/Astrology)** – motion in time

Originally articulated in Pythagorean and Platonic traditions and later preserved through medieval scholastic education (Boethius), the Quadrivium is not merely an academic curriculum. It is a **complete perceptual architecture of how consciousness learns to read reality**.

Where the Trivium (Grammar, Logic, Rhetoric) governs **how we think**, the Quadrivium governs **how reality itself is structured and perceived**.

In modern terms, the Quadrivium can be understood as:

- **Number**: Frequency, quantization, informational discreteness
- **Geometry**: Field structure, spatial intelligence, embodiment form
- **Harmony**: Phase relationships, interval, vibration, entrainment
- **Cosmos:** Cycles, orbital mechanics, rhythm of time and psyche Thus, the Quadrivium is the **scientific grammar of manifestation itself**.

## The Quadrivium as the Hidden Structure of Yoga

In this book, the Quadrivium is revealed not as an external theory but as the **hidden architecture already governing yogic practice**:

- **Number** governs breath ratios, mantra counts (108), and sequence order
- **Geometry** governs asana, spirals, arcs, axes, triangles, and load lines
- **Harmony** governs breath cadence, tonal mantra resonance, and emotional entrainment
- **Cosmos** governs timing of practice, planetary cycles, lunar tides, seasonal sadhana, and initiatory thresholds

This is why yoga, when fully matured, naturally unfolds into **sacred geometry, sound healing, numerological intelligence, and astro-cosmic awareness** without being forced.

The Quadrivium is not added onto yoga.

**It is the deep mathematical skeleton that yoga has always been expressing through the body.**

## The Quadrivium as a Science of Consciousness Coherence

At the highest level, the Quadrivium functions as a **coherence engine** that stabilizes:

- Perception
- Motion
- Thought
- Rhythm
- Ethics
- Destiny

Each limb of the Quadrivium trains the human being to **perceive reality without distortion**:

- Number trains **clarity of informational**

**perception**

- Geometry trains **structural embodiment**
- Harmony trains **resonant regulation**
- Cosmos trains **temporal and karmic orientation**

When the Quadrivium becomes fully integrated within yoga and alchemy, the result is **the Philosopher's Stone as a living human state**.

## Further Study in the Quadrivium & Consciousness Architecture

For readers drawn toward deeper study of:

- Sacred Number
- Sacred Geometry
- Planetary Harmonics
- Archeometer Science
- Consciousness Coherence
- Mathematical Cosmology

Further study is available through the original work of **Dr. Enolia Harris Pedro**:

https://enolia.live

— *Dr. Enolia Harris Pedro*

Including her authored works:

- **The Trivium: Ancient Wisdom for Modern Times** (based on the works of *Master Sister Mary Joseph*)
- **The Quadrivium of Mastery**

These texts provide the **mathematical, cosmic, and philosophical substrate** supporting the yogic-alchemical synthesis presented in this book.

# V. ALCHEMICAL-YOGIC CORRESPONDENCES (SUMMARY)

| Alchemy. | Physiology | Yogic Domain | Quadrivial Domain |
|---|---|---|---|
| Nigredo | Nervous freeze | Shadow purification | Void / Zero |
| Albedo | Respiratory circulation | Pranayama | Harmony |
| Citrinitas | Neural organization | Asana as geometry | Geometry |
| Rubedo | Cardiovascular ignition | Tapas / Bhakti | Power |
| Cauda Pavonis | Cognitive multiplicity | Lineage synthesis | Cosmos |
| Distillation | Identity coherence | Sadhana refinement | Number |
| Stone | Total integration | Yogic embodiment | Unified Logos |

# Primary Works by the Authors

## Harris Pedro, Enolia Dr.

Harris Pedro, E. (2026). *The Trivium: Ancient Wisdom for Modern Times* (Based on the works of Master Sister Mary Joseph). Enolia International Press & LaserEdulogics Educational Institute.

Harris Pedro, E. (2026). *The Quadrivium: From Numbers to Stars and the Archéomètre Within* Enolia International Press & LaserEdulogics Educational Institute.

Harris Pedro, E. (2022). *The Seven Principles of Self-Mastery.* Enolia International Press.

Harris Pedro, E. (2026). *Enolia: Finding My Sovereign Voice with My Grandmother Elder.* 3rd Edition. Enolia International Press.

Harris Pedro, E. (2022). *Discover Your*

*Sovereign Voice Journal.* Enolia International Press.

Harris Pedro, E. (2022). *Know Thyself: 30 Days to Conscious Living*. Enolia International Press.

Harris Pedro, E. (2026). *Sacred Geometry in Motion: From Number to Cosmic Consciousness.* Enolia International Press.

Harris Pedro, E. (2026). *The Sovereignty of Worth: Conscious Coherence and the True Self.* Enolia International Press.

Harris Pedro, E. (2026). *The Architecture of Communication: From Pattern to Language* Enolia International Press

Further study, leadership training, and certification available at: **https://enolia.live**

## Shearer, Tracy

Shearer, T. (2010-2019). *Yoga Girl Goes Vegan* https://yogagirlgoesvegan2.blogspot.com/

Shearer, T. (2012). *Pulp Madness, Raw Whole Food Nutrition.* Yoga Girl Goes Vegan.

Shearer, T. (2013). *Plant-Based Nutrition Curriculum. C*ornell University.

Shearer, T. (2013). *Eat Your Vitamins.* Plant Powered Living.

Shearer, T. (2019). *Getting Started, A Beginner's Guide to Plant Based Nutrition.* Yoga Girl Goes Vegan

Shearer, T. (2019). *Plant-Based Nutrition & Yogic Wellness Programs.* Flourish With Tracy.

Shearer, T. (2019). *Kaivalya Yoga Method Training Materials.* Kaivalya Yoga Method Academy.

Shearer, T. (2022). *Yogamu Institute Teaching A cademy Curriculum.* Yogamu Institute.

Shearer, T. (2022). *Global Yoga Therapy & Ayurv eda Organization (GYTA) Standards.* GYTA.
Shearer, T. (2023). *Yoga Teacher -Instructor Training Program.* Flourish With Tracy.

Further study, leadership training, and certifica tion available at:
https://www.flourishwithtracy.com

## Classical Alchemy & Hermetic Science

Valentine, B. (1600/2010). *The Twelve Keys.* Weiser Books. Paracelsus. (1530/2002). *The Archidoxes of Magic.* Inner Traditions.
Fulcanelli. (1926/1988). *The Mystery of the Cathedrals.* Samuel Weiser. Hall, M. P. (1928/2003). *The Secret Teachings of All Ages.* Tarcher.
Evola, J. (1931/1995). *The Hermetic Tradition.* Inner Traditions.
Jung, C. G. (1955–1956/1970). *Mysterium*

*Coniunctionis.* Princeton University Press.
Regardie, I. (1937/1989). *The Golden Dawn.* Llewellyn.

## Yoga, Tantra & Vedic Philosophy

Patañjali. (200 BCE/2013). *The Yoga Sutras.* (Trans. S. Satchidananda). Integral Yoga Publications.
Svātmārāma. (15th c./2002). *Hatha Yoga Pradipika.* (Trans. B. M. Singh). Motilal Banarsidass. Feuerstein, G. (1998). *The Yoga Tradition.* Hohm Press.
Iyengar, B. K. S. (1966/2005). *Light on Yoga.* Schocken. Saraswati, S. S. (1984). *Kundalini Tantra.* Yoga Publications Trust. Sivananda, S. (1956). *Science of Pranayama.* Divine Life Society.
Cope, S. (2006) *The Wisdom of Yoga, A Seeker's Guide to Extraordinary Living.* Bantom Books.
Radhanath, S. (2008) *The Journey Home, Autobiography of an American Swami.* Mandala Publishing.

Sarvananda, S. (1950) *Manduyka Upanishad.* Sri Ramakrishna Math.Prabhupada, S. (1972/1983) *Bhagavad Gita As It Is.* The Bhaktivendanta Book Trust.

Kabir. Songs of Kabir. Translated by Rabindranath Tagore. London: Macmillan, 1915.

## The Quadrivium & Classical Cosmology

Plato. (4th c. BCE/2008). *Timaeus.* Hackett Publishing.

Plato. (4th c. BCE/2007). *Republic* (Book VII). Penguin Classics.

Boethius. (6th c./1989). *De Institutione Arithmetica & Musica.* Cambridge University Press. Nicomachus of Gerasa. (2nd c./1938). *Introduction to Arithmetic.* University of Michigan Press. Kepler, J. (1619/1997). *Harmonices Mundi.* American Philosophical Society.

Guénon, R. (1946/2001). *The Great Triad.* Sophia

Perennis.

## Sacred Geometry & Harmonics

Lawlor, R. (1982). *Sacred Geometry: Philosophy and Practice*. Thames & Hudson. Critchlow, K. (1969/1983). *Order in Space*. Thames & Hudson. Doczi, G. (1981). *The Power of Limits*. Shambhala. Fuller, B. (1975). *Synergetics*. Macmillan.

## Kabbalah, Gematria & Archeometer

Saint-Yves d'Alveydre. (1903/1984). *The Archeometer*. Samuel Weiser. Kaplan, A. (1985). *Meditation and Kabbalah*. Samuel Weiser.
Scholem, G. (1941/1974). *Major Trends in Jewish Mysticism*. Schocken.
Abellio, R. (1965/1984). *The Structure Absolue*. Archè Edidit.
Fabre d'Olivet. (1815/1991). *The Hebraic Tongue Restored*. Inner Traditions.

## Indigenous Cosmology & Oral Traditions

*(Cited as Living Lineages, Not Extracted Texts)*

Ojibwa Medicine Traditions (Oral Transmission) Lakota Sundance & Cosmology (Oral Transmission) Toltec & Yaqui Wisdom Lineages (Oral Transmission) Hopi Prophetic Teachings (Oral Transmission)

Q'ero Andean Cosmology (Oral Transmission)

Ovimbundu Cosmology of Angola (Oral Transmission) Mapuche Cosmology of Chile (Oral Transmission) Luhya Elders of Kenya (Oral Transmission)

Waitaha Lineage of Aotearoa (Oral Transmission)

## Neuroscience, Somatics & Consciousness Studies

Porges, S. (2011). *The Polyvagal Theory.* Norton. Levine, P. (2010). *In an Unspoken Voice.* North Atlantic Books. Damasio, A. (1999). *The Feeling of What Happens.* Harcourt Brace. Pert, C. (1997). *Molecules of Emotion.* Scribner.

Lipton, B. (2005). *The Biology of Belief.* Hay House.

Laszlo, E. (2007). *Science and the Akashic Field.* Inner Traditions.

## Tarot, Astrology & Cosmic Timing

Rudhyar, D. (1936/1970). *The Astrology of Personality.* Lucis. Campion, N. (2008). *A History of Western Astrology.* Continuum. Crowley, A. (1944/1996). *The Book of Thoth.* Weiser.

Case, P. F. (1947/2006). *The Tarot: A Key to the Wisdom of the Ages.* Macoy.

## Ethics of Indigenous Knowledge & Transmission

United Nations. (2007). *UN Declaration on the Rights of Indigenous Peoples (UNDRIP).*

UNESCO. (2019). *Indigenous Knowledge*

*Protection Guidelines.*

International Council of Elders. (2018). *Oral Knowledge Preservation Protocols.*

## Statement of Further Study & Certification

Advanced study in:

- Quadrivium & Trivium Pedagogy
- Archeometer & Gematria
- Sacred Geometry
- Numerological Cosmology
- Consciousness Coherence
- Empower Achieve Succeed (EAS) Coach Certification
- Indigenous-Informed Leadership

Programs is available through:

**Dr. Enolia Harris Pedro**

https://enolia.live

Including her authored works:

- *The Trivium: Ancient Wisdom for Modern Times* (based on the works of Master

Sister Mary Joseph)

- *The Quadrivium by Dr. Enolia Harris Pedro*
- *Geometry in Motion: From Number to Cosmic Consciousness*

These texts provide the **mathematical, cosmic, and philosophical substrate** underlying the synthesis in this book.

Further yogic, nutritional, breath-centered, and embodiment-based study is available through:

**Tracy Shearer – Flourish With Tracy**

https://www.flourishwithtracy.com

# CLOSING DECLARATION

This bibliography includes both documented textual lineages and living oral transmission traditions. Certain teachings referenced in this work are preserved through elder-based transmission and ceremonial trust rather than institutional publication. Their inclusion here represents acknowledgment of lineage, not extraction of intellectual property.

# INDEX

www.ingramcontent.com/pod-product-compliance
Ingram Content Group UK Ltd.
Pitfield, Milton Keynes, MK11 3LW, UK
UKHW041635190726
13854UKWH00006B/2504

9 798995 153702